Successful
SERGING

Creative Publishing international

First published in the United States of America by
Creative Publishing international, Inc., a member of
Quayside Publishing Group
400 First Avenue North
Suite 300
Minneapolis, MN 55401
1-800-328-3895

www.creativepub.com

Visit www.Craftside.Typepad.com for a behind-the-scenes peek at our crafty world!

ISBN-13: 978-1-58923-461-1
ISBN-10: 1-58923-461-8

10 9 8 7 6 5 4 3
Library of Congress Cataloging-in-Publication Data
Baumgartel, Beth.
    Successful serging : from setup to simple and specialty stitches / Beth Baumgartel.
      p. cm.
    Includes index.
    ISBN-13: 978-1-58923-461-1
    ISBN-10: 1-58923-461-8
    1. Serging. I. Title.

TT713.B357 2009
646.2'044--dc22

2009015840

Technical Editor: Carol Fresia
Proofreader: Kathleen Dragonlich
Book Design: Heather Lambert
Page Layout: Heather Lambert
Illustrations: Heather Lambert
Sample Maker: Pamela Leggett
Printed in China

Successful
SERGING

From Setup to Simple and Specialty Stitches

BETH BAUMGARTEL

Contents

Why Choose a Serger?

For the speed and the many creative possibilities, of course!

Modern sergers are easy to use and capable of so much more than edge finishing—which was their great appeal when they first appeared on the market. They are still great for finishing seam allowances for a professional, ready-to-wear look. They also stitch flat, smooth seams in hard-to-sew knits and slippery fabrics.

Today's machines are also capable of stitching with many threads at once, in a variety of styles, which gives you incredible potential for creating decorative work. Flatlocking, couching, rolled hems, beading, and novelty-thread work are just a few of the many possibilities. Creative potential is the reason that the serger is the machine everyone is talking about and wants to own!

The question is not whether you should invest in a serger (because you really should!), but how you can use your serger to its full potential. This book is filled with serging tips and techniques to help you answer that question. In this easy-to-use reference, you'll learn how to make the most of the time you spend sewing—regardless of the type of sewing you do or how much of it—so you can create the very best projects possible. So, serge on!

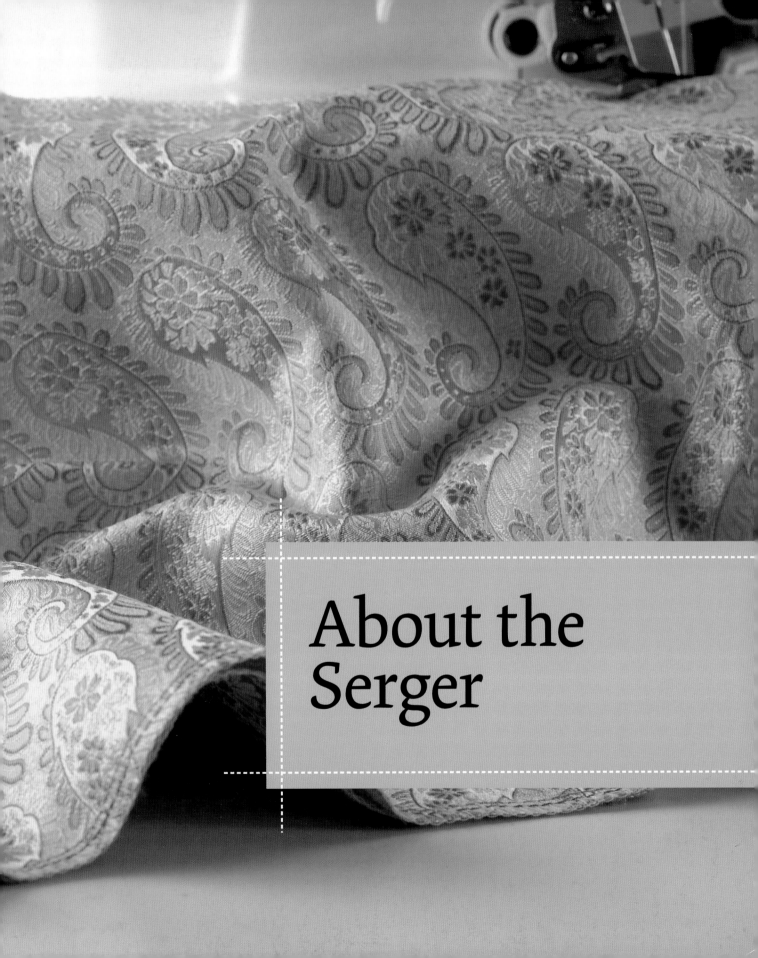

About the Serger

What Is a Serger?

A serger is also called an overlock or Merrow machine (the manufacturer of the industrial version). Overlock is really the name of the primary stitch formed by the machine, but the term is frequently used to describe the machine itself.

The serger stitches a seam while trimming and overcasting the seam allowance, all in one step. It moves at a speed of about 1,700 stitches per minute—much faster than a standard home sewing machine. It can save hours of tedious seam finishing and give all your projects a more professional look, whether the serged stitches are functional (on the inside) or decorative (on the outside)!

A serger is typically defined by the number of threads it uses, anywhere from two to five (with additional threads if there are double or triple needles on a single shaft). The number of threads, in turn, determines how many stitches and what types of stitches the machine can form. (For a complete explanation of serger stitches, see pages 44–55.)

Sergers have been marketed to home sewers for only about 35 years. The original machines were large, heavy, and loud, with exposed knives that were somewhat dangerous. Today's sergers are much more user-friendly and are available at many price points and with a range of features. Many models are computerized.

A serger can't entirely replace a sewing machine, but it can certainly enhance your overall sewing. You will find that the more you use your serger, the more comfortable and knowledgeable you will become, and the more you'll be able to do with it. Whatever you call it—the *serger*, *Merrow*, or *overlock* machine—once you start using it, you'll wonder how you ever did without it.

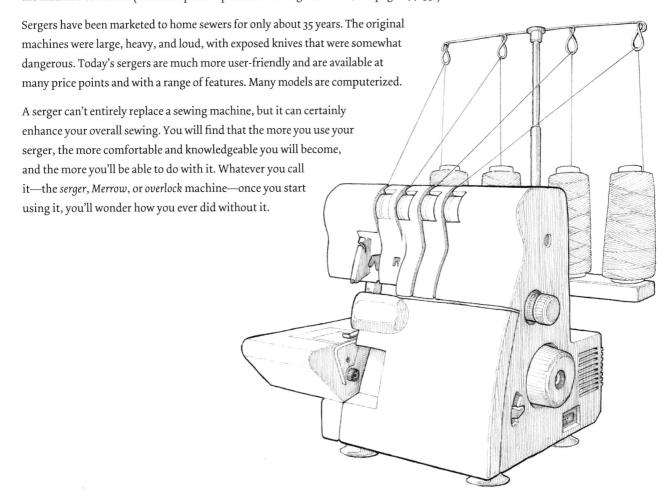

THE SERGER AND THE SEWING MACHINE

The serger is the perfect complement to your sewing machine—for its speed, its professional edge finishing, and its decorative versatility. Although it can't replace a sewing machine, you can sew entire projects on a serger, such as knit items and some home décor projects.

The biggest difference between a sewing machine and a serger is that sergers have loopers instead of a bobbin for the lower thread. The thread passes through large eyes on the loopers, instead of wrapping around them, as it would around the bobbin. You still need your sewing machine to sew facings, most zippers, buttonholes, topstitching, and tailoring. The sewing machine is essential when accuracy, precision, and garment fit are important.

You don't absolutely need a serger, of course—unless you sew professionally—but a serger certainly makes your sewing life easier, your finished projects more professional looking, and the sewing experience much more fun.

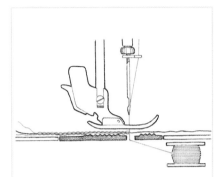

A sewing machine forms a stitch when the thread from a single needle (or multiple needles on the same needle shaft) pierces the fabric and interlaces with the thread from a bobbin, located within the bed of the machine.

SEWING MACHINE AND SERGER FEATURES

SEWING MACHINE

❖ 1 or 2 spools of thread, plus one bobbin

❖ Lower thread feeds from a single bobbin.

❖ Threads penetrate fabric.

❖ Machine can backstitch.

❖ Makes professional buttonholes.

❖ Stitches precisely on curves and corners.

❖ Does not trim seam allowances.

SERGER

❖ 2 to 10 spools of thread

❖ Lower thread feeds through loopers.

❖ Threads penetrate and/or wrap around fabric edge.

❖ Machine cannot backstitch.

❖ Making buttonholes is challenging.

❖ Is challenging to stitch precisely on corners and curves.

❖ Trims seam allowances as it stitches.

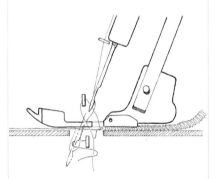

A serger forms stitches with multiple threads. The serger has one, two, or three long metal loopers that carry the threads over and under the fabric. The loopers form stitches around the edge of the fabric without penetrating it. The looper threads interlace with the needle threads, which do penetrate the fabric.

SERGER CAPABILITIES

When you buy a serger, take it out of the box right away and get acquainted. The more you work with your serger, the more you will discover all that it can do. The serger's stitch capabilities depend on the number of threads the serger can accommodate and the number of loopers it has. Regardless of the number of threads, however, most sergers are capable of the following tasks:

❖ Applying professional-looking seam finishes

❖ Sewing and finishing long, straight seams in a single pass

❖ Stitching a two-thread chain stitch

❖ Sewing narrow pintucks

❖ Creating decorative lettuced edges

❖ Some straight stitching for garment construction

❖ Making decorative trim

❖ Working with difficult-to-sew fabrics (including stretch knits)

❖ Strengthening children's clothing (and other garments subject to wear and tear)

❖ Adding decorative edgestitching to reversible items

❖ Working with decorative and heavy threads (easily threaded through the loopers)

❖ Executing beautiful rolled edges and hems (perfect for table linens and eveningwear)

❖ Stitching pucker-free seams and edge finishes

❖ Gathering single layers of fabric and gathering one fabric to another

❖ Feeding fabric layers evenly through the machine to match plaids, stripes, and patterns

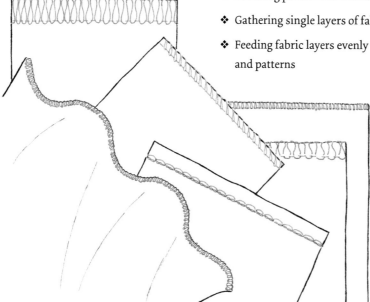

❖ Decorative stitching for unique accent pieces and creative fabric "painting"

❖ Doing all the stitching quickly, leaving more time for creative work!

ANATOMY OF THE SERGER

At first glance, a serger may look unusual and a little intimidating, but looks can be deceiving! Although every serger model is slightly different, the most essential parts on all machines are the same. The serger's mechanical parts and the computer (if the machine is computerized) reside inside the body of the serger, but you don't have access to them.

Sergers start to look different from each other on the front of the machine—depending both on the manufacturer and the machine's maximum number of threads.

THREAD GUIDE POLE, THREAD GUIDES, AND SPOOL PINS

Vertical spool pins on the back of the machine hold the thread spools or cones. Each thread travels from the spool through a thread guide on the top of a telescoping thread pole. The pole prevents the threads from tangling and helps them feed evenly into the tension dials. The thread pole should be fully extended during stitching and can be lowered for easier storage.

HAND WHEEL

The hand wheel lowers and raises the needles, so it's possible to form stitches manually whenever necessary. If there isn't an arrow printed directly on the hand wheel indicating the correct direction, check the owner's manual. Turning the wheel in the wrong direction leads to tangled and broken threads.

POWER SWITCH AND FOOT CONTROL

Most machines have a power switch on the lower right side of the machine that turns the machine and light on. (Older machines turn on as soon as they are plugged in.) There's also a socket for the power cord and foot control. On some machines, the foot pedal controls the speed of the machine; others have a dial or slide setting that offers steady and variable speeds. By adjusting the speed control, you can control the speed of the stitching, regardless of how much pressure you put on the foot pedal.

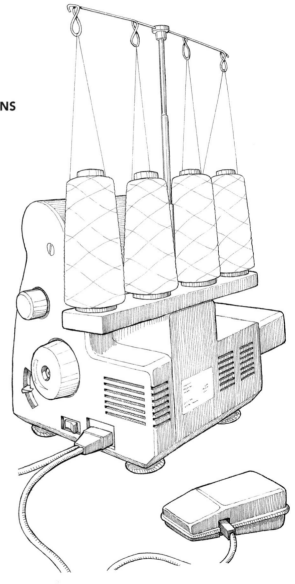

WORK SPACE

Like sewing machines, sergers vary as to how much space they provide to the left and right of the needle. If you frequently work with large pieces of fabric and need to sew away from the edge of the fabric, extra room between the needle and the body of the serger is a definite plus.

THREAD GUIDES

Helpful color-coded thread guides and paths are printed on the body of the machine. These guides make threading easier.

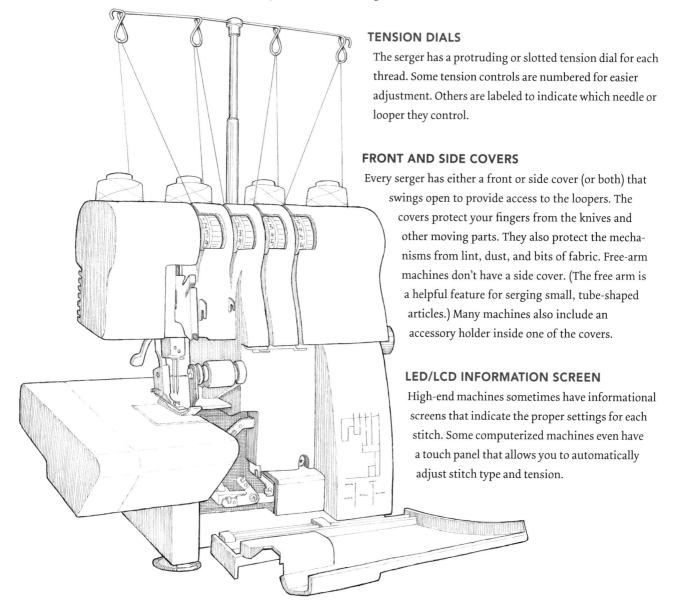

TENSION DIALS

The serger has a protruding or slotted tension dial for each thread. Some tension controls are numbered for easier adjustment. Others are labeled to indicate which needle or looper they control.

FRONT AND SIDE COVERS

Every serger has either a front or side cover (or both) that swings open to provide access to the loopers. The covers protect your fingers from the knives and other moving parts. They also protect the mechanisms from lint, dust, and bits of fabric. Free-arm machines don't have a side cover. (The free arm is a helpful feature for serging small, tube-shaped articles.) Many machines also include an accessory holder inside one of the covers.

LED/LCD INFORMATION SCREEN

High-end machines sometimes have informational screens that indicate the proper settings for each stitch. Some computerized machines even have a touch panel that allows you to automatically adjust stitch type and tension.

NEEDLE AND NEEDLE CLAMP

One to five needles will fit into the needle clamp, but you usually use only one, two, or three at a time. The needles are held in place with a "set" screw. Your machine is equipped with a small screwdriver that facilitates removing and inserting the needles. For decorative stitching with multiple threads, you can sometimes mount twin needles on a single shaft.

PRESSER FOOT AND PRESSER FOOT LIFTER

The presser foot holds down the fabric. Every machine is equipped with an all-purpose presser foot and usually one or two novelty feet that snap on and off (or, on older machines, screw on and off). (For more about novelty feet, see page 21.) A lever located on the body of the machine lifts the foot.

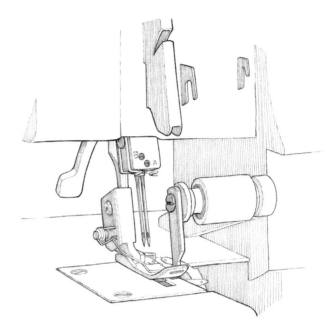

NEEDLE PLATE AND FEED DOGS

The needle plate surrounds and protects the feed dogs. The feed dogs are the parallel metal tracks that protrude through the needle plate on the work surface of the serger. The feed dogs—which are much longer and higher than those on a standard sewing machine—move the fabric through the serger. One set of feed dogs is in front of the needle; the other set is behind it. The adjustment of their relative speeds causes the dogs either to ease or stretch the fabric as it's being stitched.

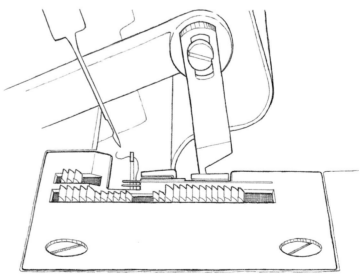

LOOPERS (TWO OR THREE)

Every serger has two loopers: An upper looper feeds the thread that lies on top of the fabric, and a lower looper feeds the thread that lies on the bottom of the fabric. Five-thread sergers have a third looper. Doors or covers provide access only to the loopers and any of the stitch regulators that are located inside the machine.

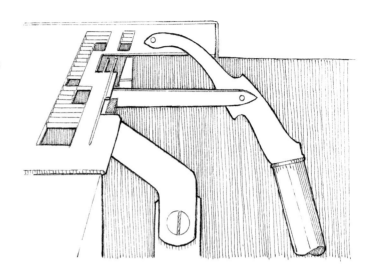

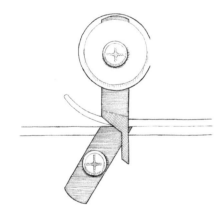

UPPER AND LOWER KNIVES

The serger's two knives work together like scissors to trim the fabric as the machine stitches. The upper knife is visible in front of the needle. It moves in an up-and-down motion against the fixed lower knife, which is located just below the needle plate. On many machines, the upper knife can be disengaged for decorative stitching.

The lower knife is stationary and is located just to the right of and level with the feed dogs. On some machines you can adjust the position of the lower knife to change the stitch width (see page 36).

STITCH FINGER

The stitch finger is part of either the needle plate or the presser foot. It supports the thread as the stitches are formed and prevents the fabric from curling. Some machines have a separate, interchangeable needle plate with a narrower stitch finger for sewing a rolled hem.

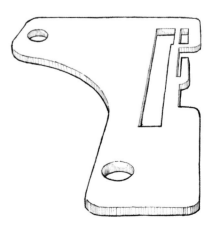

STITCH REGULATORS AND CONTROLS

In addition to the thread tension dials, there are four main stitch regulators, or controls, that affect the look and quality of the stitches. Depending on the serger, these controls can be inside or outside the machine. Each is examined in depth in the chapter on serger setup (see pags 34–37).

stitch-length regulator:

This dial or lever adjusts the amount of fabric that moves through the machine as the stitches are formed—which, in effect, determines how much thread extends across the surface of the fabric. Usually the higher the stitch length number, the longer the stitch, and the more fabric you see between stitches. Sometimes the regulator is inside the machine, which makes it more difficult to change the stitch length while you're stitching. On most new machines, this control is located somewhere on the exterior of the machine.

cutting-width regulator:

The cutting width, also called the stitch width, refers to the width of the fabric under the thread loops. You can change the width by turning a dial or by selecting either the right or left needle. The dial or regulator actually moves the knives so they cut more or less of the fabric edge. Often there is an "N" on the dial to indicate a normal setting. On some older machines, you need to change the needle plate to change the stitch width.

differential-feed control:

This dial or lever, found on the exterior of the machine, controls the relative speeds of the front and back sets of feed dogs. Adjusting both feed dogs prevents the fabric from stretching (knits) or puckering (sheers) during stitching. (Older machines may not have this feature.)

The adjustment dial is marked differently on all machines, but there is usually an "N" or a **1** to indicate the normal setting; the other settings are marked on either side.

presser foot pressure adjustor:

Not every machine has an adjustment for presser foot pressure, especially if the serger has a differential feed adjustment. It controls the amount of pressure on the fabric from the presser foot. If there is a dial or lever, it's usually on the top of the serger. Some machines have a screw that can be tightened or loosened. If possible, avoid changing the screw—it can be hard to get it back to its normal, factory-set setting.

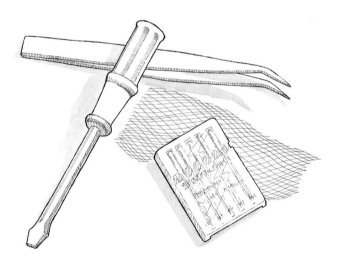

Most machines are sold with a small accessory case, which may fit within the body of the machine for easy storage. The kit usually contains a screwdriver, an extra lower knife, thread spool caps, thread cone adaptors, thread nets, an oiler, tweezers, a looper threader, extra needles, and a brush to clean the machine.

NEEDLES

A serger forms stitches with one, two, or three needles at a time, depending on the type of stitch. The shank is the upper part of the needle, which fits into the needle clamp. The shaft is the lower half of the needle. It has a long groove cut into the front to provide a channel for the thread and a scarf, a tiny notch on the back of the needle, near the tip.

Double needle

TYPES OF NEEDLES

Most sergers accept standard sewing machine needles, but some sergers require industrial needles and sometimes even custom needles. Refer to your owner's manual to be sure you have the correct needles. Different brands are not usually interchangeable.

The shank of the standard needle has a flat side. Insert the needle with the flat side toward the back of the machine. Industrial needles have a round shank, so take care to insert this type with the groove facing toward the front of the machine.

NEEDLE SIZE AND STYLE

Working with the right size and style of needle minimizes potential stitch problems. Needle size refers to the diameter of the needle: The larger the number, the larger the needle. Choose different size needles to accommodate various thread widths.

SELECTING NEEDLES	
NEEDLE SIZE	**BEST FABRIC, THREAD, OR USE**
10/70	Lightweight fabrics and fine threads; avoid using a needle smaller than 10/70 because stitches won't form properly.
11/75 or 12/80	Medium-weight fabrics and most standard serging
14/90	Heavyweight fabrics and thicker, decorative threads
16/100 or larger	Very thick decorative threads; test first to make sure the needle doesn't touch the upper looper during stitching (see page 19).
NEEDLE STYLE	**BEST FABRIC, THREAD, OR USE**
Universal	Works for most fabrics and standard serging
Sharp	Tightly woven fabrics that require an extra sharp, penetrating needle
Ballpoint	Knits
Topstitch	Heavyweight and denim fabrics
Embroidery	Novelty threads (larger, coated eye prevents thread breakage)
Double needle (see above)	Two needles on a single shaft (for decorative stitching)

TROUBLESHOOTING

If your stitch doesn't look quite right, the problem might be the needle. Because of the high speed of serging, needles get old and dull and develop little nicks quickly, so you need to replace them regularly. Needles also become dull more quickly when you serge synthetic or metallic fabrics.

Before you replace the needle, check to be sure that the original one is inserted properly. The problem could simply be a matter of incorrect installation. Every machine is slightly different, so refer to your owner's manual.

If replacing the needle doesn't improve the quality of your stitch, try another new needle, just in case the replacement needle was defective. If you're working with more than one needle, make sure they are the same size. Be sure to remove any needles that you don't need for the stitch you are forming. Most machines come with a small screwdriver and extra needles.

to remove the old needle: Unplug the machine from the electric outlet before you start. Turn the hand wheel so the needle is in the highest position. You usually need to loosen one or two tiny screws to remove the old needle and then retighten them to secure the new needle. Grasp the old needle with tweezers before loosening the screw. Loosen the screw (don't remove it completely) and gently pull the needle down out of the clamp.

to insert the new needle: Push the new needle up into the needle clamp as far as it will go (if it's not all the way up, the machine won't stitch properly). On most sergers, the right and left needles sit at different depths in the needle clamp, so you can't always tell just from looking if they're properly seated. Trust your fingers to tell you if the needle is inserted fully into the clamp.

WORKING WITH LARGE NEEDLES

When stitching with thick, decorative threads, you might need to install a larger needle than usual. To check that the needle isn't too large for your serger, unthread the machine and insert the needle. Slowly turn the hand wheel and listen as the looper passes the needle. Make sure you don't hear any noises and that the needle and looper don't touch. If all is quiet and the two don't touch, go ahead and serge with the large needle. Otherwise, thread the heavier thread in the loopers (see page 26).

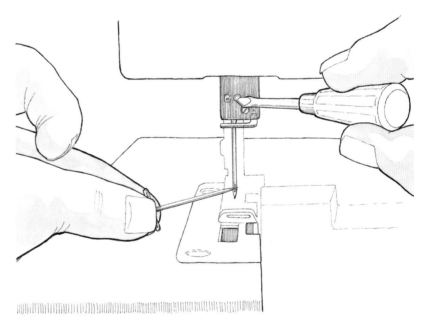

To more easily maneuver a new needle into the needle clamp, put a toothpick or T-pin into the eye of the needle. Once the shank is in the hole, push upward gently to make sure the needle is inserted all the way.

KNIVES

The knives, also called the cutting blades, are a big part of what makes sergers so great to work with. They trim the fabric even before the stitches are formed to create a nice, neat, finished edge. They're one reason why serging saves you so much time—you'll never have to hand-trim seam allowances again.

The two knives are positioned in front of the needle. The lower knife is stationary during stitching. The upper knife moves up and down against the lower blade, creating an action similar to scissors. The lower knife wears out quickly and should be replaced three or four times a year, depending on how often you serge. The upper knife is more durable and can last several years.

WORKING WITH THE KNIVES

By disengaging the knives, you can serge away from the fabric edge, serge elastic in place without cutting through it, topstitch, and add decorative trim. By moving the lower knife side to side, you can change stich width.

There are many decorative serging options available when the knives are disengaged, but it's important to read your owner's manual and find which are suitable for your machine and its stitches.

REPLACING THE LOWER KNIFE

Raise the upper knife to its highest position. Loosen, but don't remove, the screw that holds the lower knife in place. Remove the knife and insert the new knife so the top is level with the needle plate. Retighten the screw. Turn the hand wheel several times to make sure the knives work together smoothly.

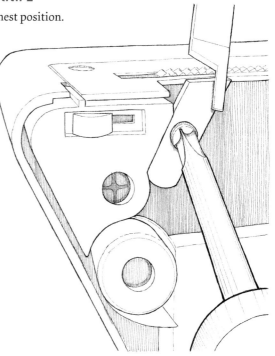

KNIFE CARE

- Never hit pins with the blades. Pins can nick or dislodge the blades.

- Clean the knives regularly with rubbing alcohol and a cotton swab to remove dust and lint.

- Synthetic fabrics cause knives to wear out more quickly than natural fiber fabrics do, so you might have to replace the lower knife after sewing synthetics.

- If the knives seem dull, don't try to sharpen them. Instead, replace the lower knife. Most machines are sold with at least one new lower knife. You can replace the lower knife yourself by referring to your owner's manual; but if you need to replace the upper knife, take the serger to a dealer.

- If the trimmed edge appears to be ragged, you probably need to change the lower knife. Before you do, check that the screw that holds the lower knife is tight; it can loosen with a fabric jam or collision with a pin.

PRESSER FEET

As there are for sewing machines, there are many special-purpose presser feet for sergers. Most simply snap on and off the machine and make a variety of specific tasks very easy.

STANDARD PRESSER FOOT

The standard foot comes with the serger. It might have built-in cording or tape guides. These guides help you apply trim and elastic and are very helpful for decorative serging.

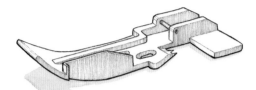

PIPING FOOT

The grooved bottom in the piping foot makes it possible to serge over zippers and attach piping, cording, and welting.

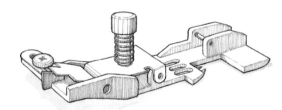

ELASTIC FOOT

The elastic foot has a screw on top. The screw enables you to attach elastic to the fabric with the correct amount of tension.

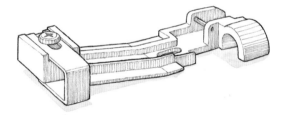

BEADING FOOT OR PEARL/SEQUIN FOOT

The beading foot has guides that fit over trim, allowing the presser foot to stay flat on the fabric as the trim is stitched in place.

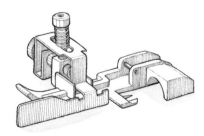

BLIND HEM FOOT

This foot sews an invisible seam or hem. It's also perfect for sewing cuffs on knit fabrics, flatlocking, and serging anytime the knives are disengaged.

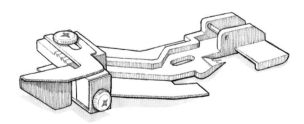

SHIRRING FOOT

This special foot gathers a single layer of fabric. It also allows you to sew together two fabrics while gathering only the bottom fabric.

Serger Thread

There are many wonderful threads you can use for serger sewing, and new ones are introduced all the time. Your choice of thread really depends on the type of fabric you are serging and the look you want to achieve. No matter what thread you choose, be sure it's of good quality. Inexpensive thread breaks easily, stitches unevenly, and causes lint buildup in the tension disks.

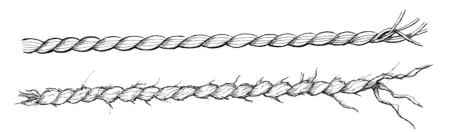

Good-quality thread is smooth, without lumps or protruding thread fibers. The irregularities found in poor-quality thread affect the appearance of the stitch. They slow the thread as it passes through the thread guides and tension disks and distort the thread tension, which in turn distorts the stitch. Look at several different threads under a magnifying glass and you will see clearly the difference in thread quality: Good-quality thread looks smooth; poor-quality thread looks hairy.

Some threads are intentionally irregular in texture. These threads are great for decorative stitching, but are threaded only through the loopers. Stick with smooth threads for the serger needles.

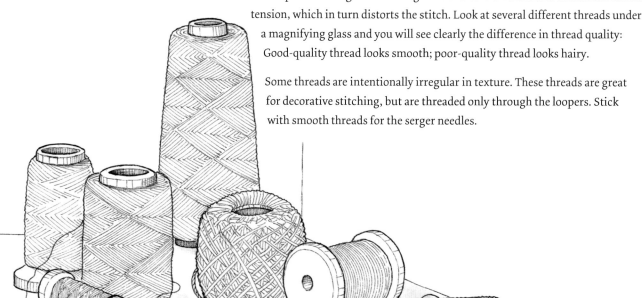

BUYING THREAD

Thread designed for serging is finer than regular sewing machine thread, yet it's strong enough to withstand the high speed of serger sewing. This feature is especially important because there are multiple threads in every serging stitch. If the thread is too thick, the seam or edge finish can be heavy and bulky. The most widely available serger thread is 100 percent polyester. It comes in many colors and is elastic, strong, and supple.

Like all-purpose sewing thread, serger thread comes in many fibers, a myriad of colors, and lots of novelty styles. As a general rule, choose basic serger thread for most types of serger sewing. If you're having a difficult time matching color, however, you can opt for all-purpose sewing thread in the needles. When you are serging decoratively, you can work with any thread, yarn, or ribbon that fits through the loopers. Serger thread cones are a good value, but don't use serger thread for garment construction. It's strong enough for overlock seams, but not for garment seams.

CONES

Serger thread is usually sold on cones, which hold 1,000–6,000 yards (914–5,486 m) of thread. The thread is cross-wound on the cones so that it feeds smoothly through the machine.

Most sergers have cone adaptors that help the thread cones fit the spool pins snugly, so the thread comes off the cone evenly. If the cones are too large for the spool pins, place them on the table behind the serger or on a separate thread cone holder. If thread is catching on the cone, file the rough area with an emery board or throw the cone away. Snagged thread causes skipped and uneven stitches. If the thread is slippery and slides off the cone, place a thread net (usually included in the accessory set) over the spool and fold the top edge back over itself so the thread doesn't get caught.

SPOOLS

Serger thread is typically sold on large cones, but that doesn't mean that you can't serge with small spools, tubes, thread wound onto sewing machine bobbins (see page 25), or even with yarn wrapped to form a ball. Conventional thread spools don't hold as much thread. It's most efficient to use them in the needles, which don't use as much thread as the loopers. If possible, choose spools with cross-wound thread and stitch slowly. Place a thread cap over a conventional thread spool to help feed the thread better. Put the spool on the pin with the notch side down so thread doesn't catch on the notch. Cone holders aren't usually necessary for spools.

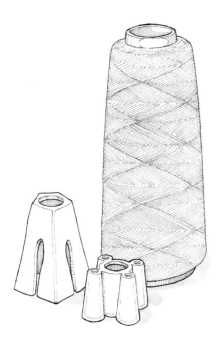

COLOR AND WEIGHT

Serger thread is available in many colors, but for most serging you can get by with just a few. All you really need are black or gray cones for dark fabrics and white or cream for light-color fabrics. Working with just a few basic shades minimizes the need to rethread for each new project.

BLENDING COLORS

As you do more serging, you might also want to have sets of cones in navy, medium gray, and red. These colors blend with almost any fabric shade or print. If you are working on a project for which a close color match is important, choose a thread color that matches or is one or two shades darker than the dominant color in the fabric. A lighter shade is more noticeable.

You don't have to match all the threads in the serger when forming a stitch. Match the left-most needle thread to the fabric. Use any reasonably close color of serger thread for the right needle and loopers.

THREAD SIZE AND WEIGHT

Smooth, fine thread is the key to smooth, flat seams. Many thread spools are marked on the side with a set of numbers: The smaller the numbers, the heavier the threads. The first number refers to the weight. The second number refers to the number of thread plies that are twisted together.

A common thread size is 40/2. In this case, 40 km (25 miles) of thread weighs 1 kg (2.2 pounds). The second number indicates that there are two plies of thread twisted together to form the strand. As a general rule, three-ply thread is best suited for garment construction because it is strong—although the type of garment, fabric weight, and type of stitch are always considerations. Two-ply thread is best for decorative use.

TIP

You can economize on thread by winding thread on sewing machine bobbins for the serger needles. Use the spools for the loopers.

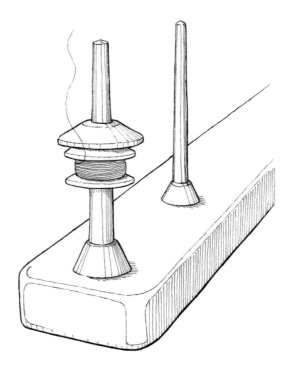

DECORATIVE THREADS

Choosing thread should be fun. There are so many beautiful threads on the market, and, with a little imagination, you can do so much with them. For functional stitching, you can stick to conventional serger threads, but switch to some of the decorative threads when your stitches will show in the finished project.

COTTON SERGER THREAD

This 100 percent cotton thread is the only natural-fiber thread made for sergers. It's soft and strong, but it has a tendency to shrink. It's best for light- or medium-weight natural-fiber fabrics. Cotton thread can be mercerized or glazed for high luster, increased strength, and reduced tendency to form lint.

COTTON-WRAPPED POLYESTER OR 100 PERCENT POLYESTER SEWING THREAD

Use polyester thread in the needles when stitching seams, especially when you can't find serger thread to match your fabric.

EMBROIDERY FLOSS

Floss is available in cotton, rayon, and silk. The plied strands can be wound onto a bobbin or left as a rope (you'll have to watch it as it feeds).

MACHINE-EMBROIDERY THREAD

This type of thread has a high sheen and silky appearance. It's suitable for decorative stitching but not for construction. It can fade over time, but is heat-resistant. It's an excellent choice for rolled-hem edges. Thread it in needles and loopers. Polyester thread is durable and colorfast; rayon thread is softer.

METALLIC THREAD

The best quality metallic thread has a nylon core for strength and an outer coating to reduce friction. Install a size 14, 16, or metallic needle when working with metallic thread.

NYLON SERGER THREAD

Nylon thread is very strong and is often used to stitch sportswear. This type of thread can be stiff, sometimes loses color, and melts at high temperatures. You'll find nylon serger thread in clear or colored monofilament or textured varieties. It works in needles and loopers.

PEARL COTTON

This heavy thread requires loose tension settings. You can buy it on cones, and it is available in several weights. Thread it only in the upper looper.

POLYESTER SERGER THREAD

Sold on cones for standard and decorative serging, polyester thread is durable, strong, heat-resistant, and colorfast. It also quickly recovers its stretch and shape. Polyester thread can be matte or glossy and is available as monofilament, smooth, or textured.

RIBBON

Thread soft, narrow ribbon, 1/16″ to 1/8″ (2 to 3 mm) wide, in the upper looper. Ribbon thread is a specialty product that lies flat and is easier to use than ribbon.

SILK THREAD

Silk produces a luxurious, shiny stitch, but is very expensive. It's also not easy to find. Search online for an assortment of colors and weights.

WOOLY NYLON

This fluffy thread comes in solid and variegated colors and in metallics. The surface can be smooth or textured (textured thread fills in nicely for decorative stitching). It offers good stretch and recovery, so it's a good choice when sewing swimwear, knits, activewear, and rolled hems. You can thread it in needles and loopers. Nylon melts, so press stitched fabrics at low temperature with a press cloth.

YARN

Yarn is heavy, so it must be threaded only in the loopers. It's great for decorative edgings on sweaters, jackets, blankets, and other projects. Avoid yarns that break easily, are very heavy, or might leave filaments in the tension disks. Two-ply baby yarn is a good choice.

WORKING WITH DECORATIVE THREADS

As soon as you serge on the right side of a project, you'll see why decorative threads are so appealing. They might call for special treatment, but the result is worth it!

❖ Decorative thread is expensive, so save it for the upper looper, which shows on the right side of the fabric. If both sides of the fabric show, thread both loopers with decorative thread.

❖ Serge on a scrap of your project's fabric first to make sure the tension and stitch settings are perfect.

❖ Decorative threads usually require looser thread tension.

❖ If the thread is temperamental, thread it through the upper looper only because it has fewer thread guides than the lower looper.

❖ If the thread is thick, make sure it can pass through the eyes of the loopers.

❖ Make sure the weight and texture of the thread, as well as the care requirements, are compatible with the fabric. For example, don't use a heavy thread on a fine, tightly woven fabric.

❖ As you begin stitching, watch the stitch finger to make sure the stitches are forming properly, especially when you are starting with new thread and don't have a chain of stitches started. It also helps to pull all the threads under and to the back of the presser foot. Use a pin to help pull the threads to the back.

❖ Stitch slowly. If you have trouble with the first few stitches, start the seam by turning the hand wheel a few rotations to get going. Lift the presser foot and place the fabric edge under it to begin the seam.

WORKING WITH DECORATIVE THREADS

THREAD TYPE OR FIBER	NEEDLE	U LOOPER	L LOOPER	TENSION
40-weight embroidery thread/rayon	yes	yes	yes	tighter
Embroidery floss/cotton	no	yes	no	looser
Fine metallic/rayon	yes	yes	might fray	normal
Heavy metallic/rayon or poly	no	yes	sometimes	looser
Monofilament/nylon	yes	yes	yes	normal
Pearl cotton	no	yes	no	looser
Ribbon/silk, polyester, rayon	no	yes	no	looser
Serger thread/polyester	yes	yes	yes	normal
Textured polyester	yes	yes	yes	looser
Wooly nylon	yes	yes	yes	looser
Yarn	no	yes	no	looser

The chart will guide you in working with decorative threads. It explains the threading options (in needle, upper looper, or lower looper) and the tension adjustments for each type. Experimentation is always essential, however. Test your thread and tension settings on scrap fabric before beginning to work on your project.

Threading Made Easy

The only difficult part of threading a serger is getting past the notion that it's difficult. Of course, every serger is different, so it's a really good idea to practice threading any serger that you are considering buying. If you do, you'll feel completely confident by the time you get your serger home. Always take your time and work methodically, consulting the owner's manual as needed.

Most sergers are pre-threaded at the factory, so when you open the machine you can see the threading paths. Sergers also have color-coded thread paths marked on the body of the serger and, usually, on a chart inside one of the doors. If the chart has numbers above the thread paths, they indicate threading order. Or you can opt to use the tying-on threading method to attach your own thread. This way, you won't have to thread the machine yourself "from scratch" until you're more familiar with the machine and ready to try. Helpful tools for threading include sharp scissors, a small magnifying glass, and tweezers.

TIP

Several manufacturers have patented self-threading systems for their sergers. Babylock's Jet-Air Threading is a pneumatic system that carries the thread through the thread path with a burst of air—worth checking out if you are in the market for a new serger.

THREADING FROM SCRATCH

These instructions are for threading a four-thread serger. It's essential that you thread in this sequence: upper looper, lower looper, right needle, left needle.

1. Extend the thread pole fully. Open the looper cover door. Remove the presser foot if you need more room to work. Rotate the handwheel so that the loopers do not cross (top) as shown.

2. Release the tension from the threads. Depending on your machine, the release methods may require manipulating a tension-release lever, lifting the presser foot, or turning the tension dials to zero. (Consult your owner's manual for specific instructions.) Check that the thread feeds smoothly off the thread spools, then place the spools on the spool pins.

3. Starting with the upper looper thread, follow your machine's threading chart to take the thread first through the tension disks and thread guides, then through the eye of the upper looper. Make sure the thread slides between the two tension disks that are part of the tension slots or dials. If your machine has tension slots, check to see that the thread is actually between the disks. If your machine has tension dials, reset the tension and gently pull the thread to make sure there is some resistance.

4. Repeat step 3 for the lower looper thread. It is important that the lower looper thread is over, or in front of, the upper looper thread. If it isn't, the thread will break when you start to stitch.

5. Thread the right needle and then the left needle, following the designated thread paths.

6. When you've threaded all the loopers and needles, pull all the threads together behind and to the left of the presser foot. Hold them as you start to stitch. Serge on a piece of scrap fabric to test that you have threaded the machine correctly.

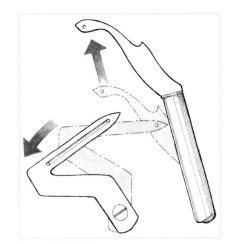

1.

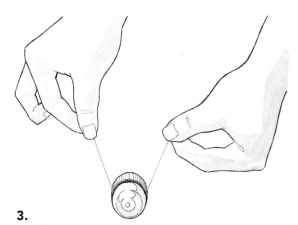

3.

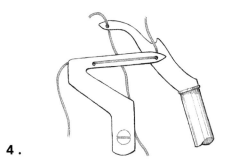

4 .

THREADING BY TYING

It's often quicker and easier to change thread color by simply tying the new thread to the old thread and pulling it through the machine. This method works especially well when you want to change just one thread.

1. Clip the needle threads just above the eye of the needles, even if you aren't changing the needle thread.

2. Hold the existing chain of stitches and run the machine until the chain consists of only the two looper threads, as shown in the drawing below.

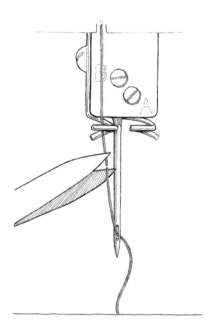

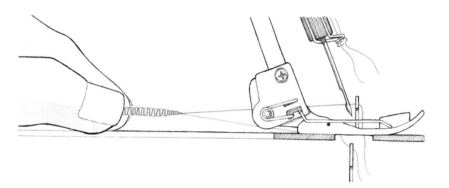

3. Cut the looper threads near the thread spools and tie the new threads to the old threads with overhand knots. Tug on the knots to tighten, then trim the thread tails to about 2″ (5 cm).

4. Turn the tension dials to zero to release tension on the threads. Be sure to note the original settings.

5. Gently pull one old looper thread from behind and to the left of the presser foot through the serger. The new thread will follow, with the knot passing through the eye of the looper. If you feel any resistance as you are pulling, stop and make sure the thread isn't caught up somewhere on the path.

6. Pull the next looper thread, and then the needle threads, as in step 5. Because you cut the needle threads above the needle eye, you will need to rethread the eyes of the needles.

7. Return the tension settings to normal. Bring all the threads together and to the back and left of the presser foot. Insert a scrap of fabric, lower the presser foot, hold the threads, and test the threading by serging on the scrap of fabric.

RETHREADING LOOPER THREADS

It's fine to rethread just the loopers. You can leave the needle threads in place. To rethread the upper looper, cut the original thread at the spool, tie on the new thread, and serge on scrap fabric until the new thread appears in the stitch. That's all you have to do.

To rethread the lower looper, start by clipping the needle threads, which wrap around the looper during stitching. Rethread the lower looper by following the thread paths or by tying on a new thread and serging on scrap fabric. This process brings the serger threads up through the throat plate. Then rethread the needles.

THREADING SUCCESS

Nine times out of ten, the reason for thread breakage and poor stitch quality is incorrect threading. Follow these steps to find the trouble spots and get back on track:

❖ Ensure that the thread pole is completely extended.

❖ Trace each thread path to make sure you haven't missed a thread guide.

❖ Make sure you threaded the loopers and needles in the proper order (see page 29).

❖ Check that the thread isn't caught on a spool notch or under the spool.

❖ Look at the tips of the needles to make sure the thread isn't wrapped around the tip.

❖ Check for tension on the thread at the tensions dials or slots (page 30).

❖ Examine the looper threads to make sure that the lower looper thread is over, or in front of, the upper looper thread (see page 29).

❖ Give a tug on the needle threads to make sure they aren't tangled in the looper threads. If they are, raise the needle as high as possible and pull the needle thread out from the needle plate with tweezers, as shown in the drawing at right.

❖ If you've checked the threading and didn't find a problem, double-check that the needles have no bends or burrs and are properly installed.

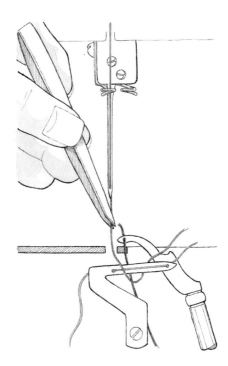

Serger
Stitches

The Perfect Stitch

Adjusting for the perfect stitch takes some practice, so it is a good idea to test your stitch before you begin every new project. Fabric, thread, and the type of stitch all affect the stitch quality. To perfect your stitch, you may have to adjust the stitch length and width, thread tension, differential feed, and presser foot pressure. Here are some guidelines to help you get the best result.

STITCH LENGTH

Stitch length is the distance between the needle penetrations along the stitching line. The distance may range from 1/50″ to 1/5″ (0.5 to 5 mm). Adjusting the stitch length is easy. Most stitch length dials have an "N" setting, which indicates a "normal" stitch length—about 10 to 14 stitches per inch (2.5 cm). This setting is suitable for medium-weight fabric and basic serging thread. You'll need to adjust the stitch length for some decorative stitches and for heavier- or lighter-weight fabric and decorative thread.

Basically, you adjust stitch length on a serger for the same reasons you would adjust it on a sewing machine. Longer stitches are best for heavier fabrics, for nonstressed seams, and for gathering. Shorter stitches are suited to lightweight fabrics and seams that will bear a lot of stress. If the fabric jams in the machine and the stitches are building up on the stitch finger, lengthen the stitch length.

If you have set the serger to a very short or very long stitch, you will probably need to adjust the tension of the looper threads (see page 43). Here are the guidelines for adjusting tension settings:

short stitches: Less thread is needed to form shorter stitches, so you need to tighten the tension to reduce extra thread. If you don't, the loops of the stitch will hang off the edge of the fabric.

long stitches: More thread is needed for a longer stitch, in order to form wider loops between needle penetrations. For a longer stitch, loosen the looper thread tensions. If you don't, the fabric edge might roll or curl under as you stitch.

STITCH LENGTH GUIDELINES

SHORTER STITCH LENGTH
(Tighten looper thread tension.)

❖ For lightweight fabrics

❖ To prevent puckering seams

❖ With fine embroidery thread

LONGER STITCH LENGTH
(Loosen looper thread tension.)

❖ For knits and heavyweight fabrics

❖ For silk and satin fabrics

❖ To prevent rippling seams

❖ With heavy, textured thread

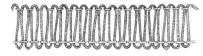

STITCH WIDTH

The stitch width, or cutting width, is the distance between the upper knife and the leftmost needle, indicated by the amount of fabric surface within the thread loops.

If the stitch width is set at 1/5″ (5 mm), then there is 1/5″ (5 mm) of fabric between the innermost stitching line and the cut fabric edge. Choose the best stitch width based on the weight of the fabric, the thickness of the thread, the stitch type, and how visible you want the stitch to be.

As a general rule, if the fabric edge curls, the stitch width is too wide. If loops of thread extend beyond the fabric edge, the stitch width is too narrow. If you are serging very heavy or very lightweight fabric or working with decorative thread, serge a test sample before you start your project. Also, keep in mind that a substantial stitch width change probably requires a tension adjustment, too (see below).

TIP

Practice serging with a normal stitch length setting and adjust it a little at a time until it is perfect.

NARROW STITCH WIDTH
(Tighten looper thread tension.)

❖ For lightweight, fine fabrics

❖ For tightly woven fabrics

❖ To prevent puckering seams

WIDER STITCH WIDTH
(Loosen looper thread tension.)

❖ For heavyweight, bulky fabrics

❖ For loosely woven fabrics and fabrics

❖ To strengthen seams

❖ To keep seam allowances flat

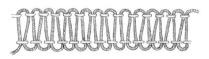

ADJUSTING THE STITCH WIDTH

There are several ways to adjust the stitch width, depending on the machine. Check your owner's manual to find out what's recommended for your specific machine.

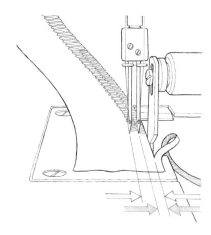

ADJUSTING THE STITCH REGULATOR

Some sergers have a cutting-width dial that actually moves the position of the lower knife (depending on your machine) closer to or farther away from the needles, so you trim more or less of the seam allowance as you serge. For a wider stitch, set the knife farther away from the needles.

CHANGING THE NEEDLE POSITION

One of the easiest ways to change the stitch width is simply to change the needle position. Use the right needle for a narrower stitch width (remove the left needle). Use the left or both needles for a wider stitch width.

CHANGING THE STITCH FINGER

Most sergers have two or more stitch fingers, including a rolled-edge stitch finger, which is very narrow. Because the stitches are formed over the stitch finger, different-width stitch fingers produce different-width stitches. Refer to your owner's manual to learn how to change or disengage the stitch finger for your specific machine. Sometimes the stitch finger is built into the throat plate or is on the presser foot. Other times, it is a removable pin, or there is an adjustment dial that moves it to the right and left.

DIFFERENTIAL FEED

The differential feed feature is standard on most new sergers—and it is a feature that is worth having. It controls the movement of the front and back feed dogs to help eliminate overstretching and wavy edges on knit fabrics and puckering in lightweight fabrics. You can also adjust differential feed settings for decorative effects such as gathering fabric, creating ruffles, and stitching a lettuce or wavy edge (see page 89).

To really understand how differential feed works, serge a knit or silk fabric scrap with the differential feed set at various settings. You'll immediately see what happens at each setting. Of course, you can manually manipulate the fabric for similar results, but it will be hard to get a consistent effect.

SETTINGS N OR 1

This marking on your machine indicates the standard or "neutral" setting for regular serging. At this setting, the front and back feed dogs work at the same speed to feed the fabric under the presser foot. There is no stretching or easing. This setting is appropriate for stable, medium-weight fabrics. On a knit fabric, this setting may produce a stretched or wavy edge. On a tightly woven fabric, it often causes puckering.

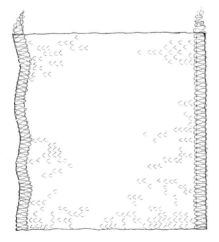

SETTING + OR 2

This setting moves the front feed dog two times faster than the rear feed dog. It helps prevent knits and stretchy fabrics from stretching. Choose this setting when serging loosely woven fabric and bias-cut edges.

This differential feed setting also allows you to gather single layer, lightweight fabrics automatically with or without a shirring presser foot. To gather or ease one length of fabric to a shorter length, install the shirring foot. Place the longer fabric piece beneath the shorter piece and pin the pieces to make sure you ease or gather the desired amount. Keep the pins away from the knife and, with the differential feed set on 2, stitch the two pieces together.

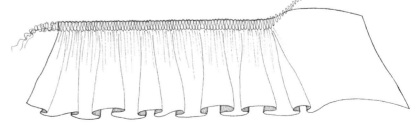

SETTING—OR 0.5 TO 0.7

This setting moves the front feed dog about half as fast as the back feed dog. It helps prevent puckering on lightweight and silky fabrics and stretches the fabric as the machine stitches. The lower the setting, the more taut the feed dogs hold the fabric. With this setting, you can create a wavy- or lettuce-edge finish.

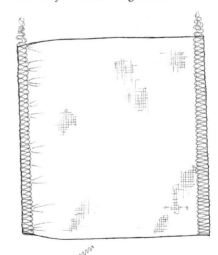

PRESSER FOOT PRESSURE

The presser foot presses down on the fabric so the feed dogs can move it through the machine. There is usually a factory preset knob, screw, or lever on the serger, near the presser foot, that adjusts the foot's pressure. When you increase the pressure, the presser foot pushes harder against the fabric surface. When you decrease the pressure, the foot eases up on the fabric. The chart below describes situations when you might need to adjust the pressure.

If you need to make a presser foot adjustment with a screw-type control, turn the screw clockwise to increase the pressure and counterclockwise to decrease it. Be sure to mark the original position on the screw before you turn it so you can return it to the original setting. On machines that have a knob or sliding lever, the original position is usually already marked. Some machines adjust the pressure of the presser foot automatically.

PRESSER FOOT GUIDELINES

INCREASE PRESSURE

❖ For lightweight fabrics

❖ For slippery, silky fabrics

❖ To prevent the fabric edge from puckering

❖ To avoid skipped stitches on heavier fabrics

DECREASE PRESSURE

❖ For heavy fabrics

❖ For bulky fabrics

❖ For fabrics with nap

❖ For sweater knits

❖ To prevent stretching along the fabric edge

> **TIP**
>
> Often you can avoid adjusting the presser foot pressure simply by adjusting the differential feed—which makes it easy to return to the normal setting.

Balancing Thread Tension

Setting the correct tension for each thread guarantees a perfect, well-balanced stitch—and it's not nearly as difficult to adjust all those controls as you might think. Some computerized sergers have an automatic tension adjustment system. Other machines provide a chart or LCD panel to suggest the correct settings for each stitch type. A little insight into how these controls work will save you from "tension" headaches!

TENSION CONTROLS

The serger has a tension knob, lay-in dial, or sliding switch for each thread. These mechanisms control the speed at which the threads move through the needles and loopers. There are two tension disks within each knob, dial, or slide, which exert pressure on the thread. The balance of tension among the threads controls the quality of the stitches.

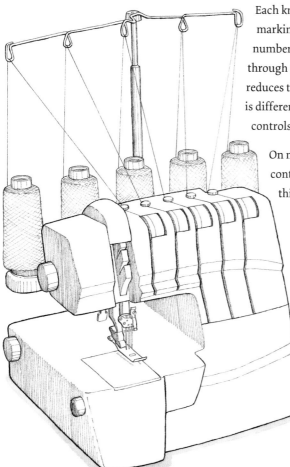

Each knob or dial controls the thread for its corresponding needle or looper. The markings, either numbers or +/– symbols, help you make adjustments. The higher number or + (positive) adjustment adds tension to the thread, so that thread passes through the machine more slowly. The lower number or – (negative) adjustment reduces the tension and allows the thread to pass through more quickly. Every serger is different, so refer to your owner's manual for a clear understanding of your tension controls.

On most machines, the two left controls are for the two needles. The two or three controls on the right are for the loopers. The positioning makes sense if you think about the stitch, which works from left to right:

- ❖ first tension control: the left needle thread
- ❖ second tension control: the right needle thread
- ❖ third tension control: the upper looper thread
- ❖ fourth tension control: the lower looper thread
- ❖ fifth tension control: the chain-stitch looper thread

In order to use and enjoy your serger to its fullest, you need to be familiar with tension adjustments. There are so many creative stitches beyond the basic three-thread overlock stitch. Don't be afraid to touch those dials!

ADJUSTING FOR THE OVERLOCK STITCH

There are many factors that affect the stitch tension, including the weight of the fabric, the type of thread, the width and length of the stitches, and the stitch style itself. Here is an overview of how to balance the tension controls for the basic overlock stitch.

All the tension controls are preset at the factory for the basic overlock stitch. You'll be making adjustments, so it's a good idea to write down the preset numbers in your owner's manual or mark them directly on the machine with a permanent marking pen. The preset settings are a good starting point for all stitches and stitch adjustments.

Turn knobs to the right to increase the tension and to the left to loosen it. Adjust vertical dials up to increase tension and down to loosen it. Move only one control at a time and in half-unit increments—balancing stitch tension doesn't require a large adjustment. When the controls are set, serge on a fabric swatch to test the stitch. If the stitch still isn't perfect, turn the control back to its original setting and try adjusting a different control. Repeat this process until you are pleased with the quality of the stitch.

Practice changing the controls to see how the changes affect the stitch. Cut a strip of scrap fabric and serge the edge, changing tension controls every few inches (centimeters) to see how the stitch changes. A very slight adjustment can really change the look. It's easier to see which thread is causing the problem if you use a different color thread for each needle and looper.

TIP

Anytime you are making tension adjustments, start with the thread that appears to be too tight. A tight thread might make the other threads appear loose when they really aren't.

PERFECT STITCH TENSION

The popular three-thread overlock stitch is basic to all serging and provides good reference for balanced threads. Here's what to look for when testing for perfect stitch tension in the overlock stitch. (Refer to the stitch glossary on pages 44–55 for examples of balanced tension for all other serger stitches.)

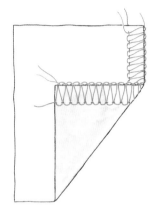

BALANCED STITCH

The needle thread resembles a row of straight stitching on the right side of the fabric and forms small dots on the wrong side. The upper and lower looper threads lie on the top and bottom of the fabric in small, even, relaxed loops that interlock at the trimmed fabric edge.

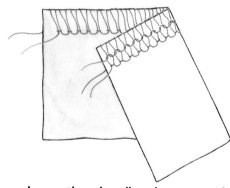

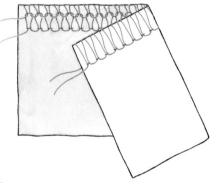

upper looper threads pull to the wrong side: The thread loops interlock on the lower surface of the fabric. To adjust, loosen the lower looper tension dial.

lower looper threads pull to the right side: The thread loops interlock on the upper surface of the fabric. To adjust, loosen the upper looper tension dial.

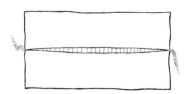

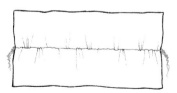

the seam pulls open: If you see a "ladder" of needle thread on the right side of the seam, tighten the needle tension or the seam will be weak and possibly pull apart.

the seam puckers: If the seam is puckered, loosen the needle tension.

TENSION ADJUSTMENTS

Adjust the primary seam thread first—the left needle if you're using a 4-thread stitch, the right needle if you're using a 3-thread stitch. Check that the seam doesn't open and form a "ladder" of visible stitches and a loose seam. If it does, tighten the tension to eliminate the ladder. If the seam puckers, loosen the thread tension. Next, adjust the other needle, if you're using one. You can almost always adjust it just as you did the other needle—or one unit tighter. Then, adjust the loopers so that the threads interlock at the edge. If you've set the needles right, you won't have to adjust them again as you work on the looper tension. Remember, the first thing to do, always, is adjust the control of the thread that appears too tight.

TIPS FOR BALANCING TENSION

❖ Rethread the machine (tension problems are almost always a threading issue).

❖ Make a test sample on the actual project fabric with the thread you plan to use. If you need to make an adjustment, you should always do it before you serge the project.

❖ Adjust one dial or knob at a time. Test the adjustment on a piece of scrap fabric. If the adjustment didn't improve the stitch, turn the dial or knob back to where it was and try again with a different dial/knob.

❖ Make very small adjustments each time and then test again.

❖ Refer to the chart below for tension adjustments for thread, fabric, and stitch length and width variations.

❖ Try a new needle if your tension adjustments don't correct the problem.

TENSION ADJUSTMENT GUIDELINES	
Condition	**Tension Adjustment**
For a wider stitch	Loosen looper tensions.
For a narrower stitch	Tighten looper tensions.
For a longer stitch	Loosen looper tensions.
For a shorter stitch	Tighten looper tensions.
For thicker fabrics	Loosen looper tensions.
For lightweight fabrics	Tighten looper tensions.
For heavy, decorative threads	Loosen all tensions.
For fine, slippery threads	Tighten all tensions.
If the seam pulls open	Tighten needle tension.
If the seam puckers	Loosen needle tension.
If loops pull to right side	Tighten lower looper or loosen upper looper.
If loops pull to wrong side	Tighten upper looper or loosen lower looper.
If there's too much needle thread on wrong side	Tighten needle tension or loosen lower looper.
If there's too much needle thread on right side	Loosen needle tension or tighten lower looper.

Basic Serger Stitches

Sergers are categorized by the number of threads they are equipped to use. Each serger makes an array of stitches, depending on the number of threads required to make them, as shown in the chart below. Some sergers can sew with as many as ten threads at one time. The most common stitches are made with two, three, four, or five threads.

STITCH TYPES

To choose the best stitch for your projects, learn a little about each type of stitch. Each stitch style has its own look and its own function.

TWO THREADS

The overedge, flatlock, and rolled-edge stitches offer additional seaming and edge-finishing options. A two-thread chain stitch looks like a standard sewing straight stitch.

THREE THREADS

The three-thread overlock is used to seam and edge-finish knits and some lightweight woven fabrics. It is also the premier edge-finishing stitch.

FOUR THREADS

A four-thread stitch is a little heavier and more secure than a three-thread stitch. The serger must have at least two needles to make most of these stitches.

FIVE THREADS

With five threads you get the most secure seam and edge-finishing stitch. The five-thread safety stitch combines the two-thread chain stitch with the three-thread overlock.

SERGER TYPES AND STITCH CAPABILITY	
Type of Serger	**Type of Stitches**
2/3 (1 needle, 2 loopers)	2-thread overedge
	3-thread overedge
	flatlock
	rolled edge
2/3/4 (2 needles, 2 loopers)	all of the above stitches
	3-thread overlock
	4-thread overlock
	4-thread mock safety
2/3/4/5 (2 needles, 3 loopers)	all of the above
	5-thread safety
	cover stitch
	chain stitch

EDGE-FINISHING STITCHES

The threads in most two-thread stitches and some three-thread stitches don't lock. The threads just interlace at or over the fabric edge. These stitches are called overedge stitches. These types of stitches aren't used for seaming; they're more suitable as edge finishing, for decorative hemming, and for finishing lightweight fabrics. You can finesse the width of an overedge stitch by using the right needle (for a narrow stitch) or the left needle (for a wider stitch).

TWO-THREAD OVEREDGE STITCH

uses: seam finish for lightweight wovens and knits

threading: one needle, one looper

stitch adjustments: Set the serger to create a balanced stitch, where the threads interlace at the fabric edge.

The two-thread overedge stitch stretches, so it's also good for finishing and hemming knit garments. A narrow overedge stitch is a good alternative to a rolled hem. Because the stitch has only two threads, it is one of the least bulky stitches, making it perfect for sheer and lightweight fabrics. You can also form a three-thread overedge, but it adds bulk.

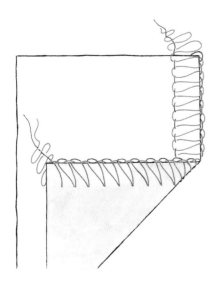

TWO-THREAD WRAPPED OVEREDGE STITCH

uses: decorative edge finish; seams for very lightweight, loose-fitting garments

threading: one needle, one looper

stitch adjustments: Increase the needle tension or loosen the looper tension so the thread wraps over to the wrong side and covers the fabric edge **(A).** Conversely, you can decrease the needle tension and increase the looper tension, and the looper thread will pull the needle thread to the front of the fabric **(B).** You can also adjust the looper tension so that the two threads lock at the needle's stitching line, which makes a more secure stitch **(C).**

The two-thread wrapped overedge is an interesting variation of the two-thread overedge. It looks just like a rolled edge, with a dense edging of thread. In fact, it is often used to duplicate the look of a rolled edge on medium- to heavy-weight fabrics. You can also stitch a three-thread wrapped overedge, but the two-thread is more suitable if you want to create a lightweight edge. (Check your owner's manual for the correct setup for your machine.)

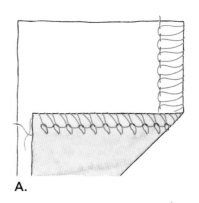

A.

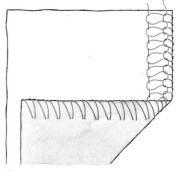

B.

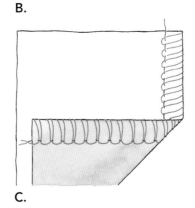

C.

ROLLED-EDGE STITCHES

A rolled edge is used almost exclusively to hem lightweight fabrics, although it can be used to seam sheer fabrics that are not subject to stress. It is the perfect hem/edge finish for lingerie, eveningwear, accessories, and table linens.

The key is the narrow stitch finger. For proper setup, refer to your owner's manual. You might need to change the presser foot or switch to a different throat plate. To stitch a rolled edge, the amount of fabric between the needle and the cut edge must be wider than the stitch finger. The fabric then rolls to the wrong side as the stitches are formed over it. Because the fabric rolls, this edge finish is most suitable for light- to medium-weight fabrics.

On heavy fabrics, use a very narrow cutting width. The fabric won't roll, so the stitch simply wraps the edge. As an alternative, you can use the wrapped overedge stitch (see page 45).

TIP

If you want good thread coverage, but a short stitch length doesn't suit your fabric, use a wooly nylon thread that fluffs up after stitching.

STITCH LENGTH AND WIDTH ADJUSTMENTS

The stitch width should be narrow. Almost all machines use the right needle (remove the left needle if your machine has one). Adjust the cutting width to fine-tune the amount of fabric into the stitches.

The stitch length should be relatively short so the thread fully covers the fabric edge. A shorter stitch length gives the appearance of a satin-stitch finish and adds some body or crispness to the fabric. A longer stitch length has a less filled-in look and a more supple hand. Choose the look you want and practice serging with different stitch lengths. If the stitch length is too short, the stitches might hang off the fabric edge; if the length is too long, the fabric might pucker.

TWO-THREAD ROLLED-EDGE STITCH

uses: narrow hem on lightweight and sheer fabrics; decorative edges; seams for sheer fabrics not subject to stress

threading: right needle and lower looper (Check your owner's manual for the correct setup for your machine.)

stitch adjustments: Tighten the needle tension until the looper thread rolls from the right side of the fabric to the wrong side, encasing the rolled fabric edge. If the thread doesn't roll all the way to the wrong side, loosen the looper tension slightly.

Although it's not as popular as the three-thread rolled edge, this stitch works beautifully on fine, lightweight fabrics. It's often the stitch of choice in home décor, evening and bridal wear, and fashion accessories. You can also use this stitch to seam sheer fabrics that are not subject to stress.

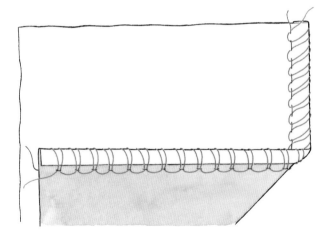

THREE-THREAD ROLLED-EDGE STITCH

uses: decorative edge finish on light- to medium-weight fabrics; edge finish on table linens, sportswear, and evening wear; seams for sheer fabrics

threading: one needle (usually the right needle) and two loopers

stitch adjustments: Tighten the lower looper tension (almost as tight as it will go) so that the upper thread wraps all the way to the wrong side of the fabric. The lower looper thread should look like a straight line of stitching on the wrong side of the fabric at the needle's stitching line. If necessary, loosen the upper looper tension, too. If the fabric puckers, loosen the needle tension ever so slightly. Always practice on scrap fabric before stitching your project.

The three-thread rolled-edge stitch is one of the most popular serger stitches. It is a one-step hem finish for fabrics that are difficult to hem traditionally. The stitch is sturdy and strong. The upper looper thread is most visible, so choose that thread color carefully. The three-thread rolled-edge stitch is a little heavier than the two-thread version, so it's suitable for use on light- to medium-weight fabrics.

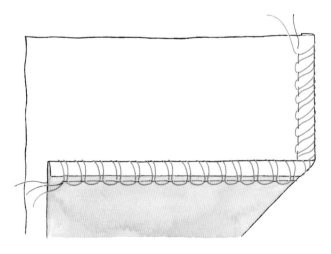

TIP
If the fabric is too fine or soft, even for two threads, spray it with spray starch before serging.

SEAMING STITCHES

The serger can create seams that are quite different from those made by a regular sewing machine. Two of the most useful seaming stitches are the chain stitch and the flatlock stitch. The chain stitch functions like a straight stitch and can be used as a seaming stitch, with any seam allowance width. You can also use it for decorative topstitching.

The flatlock stitch is sewn with the stitches extending beyond the fabric edge. Flatlock stitches form a reversible seam when they are stitched over two fabric edges. You can also use them to create reversible topstitching by stitching them over a fabric fold. After stitching, pull the fabric layers apart so the stitches lie flat, with the seam allowances enclosed within the stitches. The looper threads form a series of loops on one side of the fabric; the needle thread looks like a ladder on the other side.

TWO-THREAD CHAIN STITCH

uses: seams; decorative topstitching; basting; chain trim

threading: one needle, one looper (varies depending on model; some have a chain stitch–specific looper)

stitch adjustments: Check your owner's manual for the correct chain-stitch setup for your machine.

You can use the chain stitch alone or you can combine it with an overedge or overlock stitch to form a stitch that both seams and finishes. Although machines vary, on most sergers this stitch requires the use of a third looper, often called the chain-stitch looper. This looper places the thread on the underside of the fabric, often in a loop or braidlike pattern. If you disengage the knife, you can chain stitch anywhere on the fabric, not just along the fabric edge.

The needle thread pierces the fabric and creates what looks like a straight stitch on the right side of the fabric. The looper thread forms chainlike loops on the wrong side. When you pull on the needle thread, the whole stitch pulls right out, which makes this stitch a good basting stitch. If seams are chain-stitched, make sure to secure their ends so the seams don't pull out. The two-thread chain stitch does not stretch, so don't choose it for knit fabrics.

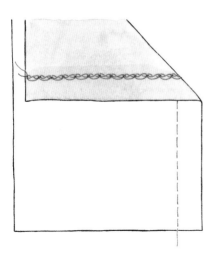

TWO-THREAD FLATLOCK STITCH

uses: seams for knits; decorative stitching; couching

threading: one needle, one looper

stitch adjustments: Set a wide, short-to medium-length, two-thread stitch with balanced stitch tension.

The two-thread flatlock stitch is less bulky than the three-thread flatlock, so it pulls flatter. The two-thread flatlock works best on medium-weight, stable fabrics. Loose weaves or unstable fabrics might stretch as you try to flatten the stitch. As you serge, make sure that the stitches hang off the fabric edge (as shown in the drawing at near right). Gently pull the fabric layers apart until the stitches lie flat.

THREE-THREAD FLATLOCK STITCH

uses: topstitching; decorative stitching; and seams for stretch knits, lingerie, and bulky fabrics, such as fake fur

threading: one needle and both upper and lower loopers

stitch adjustments: Set a wide, short-to medium-length three-thread stitch. Loosen the needle tension almost all the way and tighten the lower looper tension almost all the way. Leave the upper looper tension at the regular setting (unless you need to loosen it slightly to help pull the needle thread into position).

After making tension adjustments, serge on a piece of scrap fabric to make sure that the needle thread forms continuous Vs on the wrong side and that the lower looper forms a straight line of stitching on the right side, near the fabric edge.

Allow the stitches to extend halfway off the fabric edge. Open the fabric layers and gently pull them apart until the stitches lie flat.

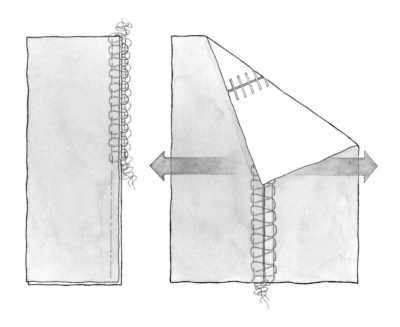

COMBINATION STITCHES

Combination stitches do more than one job: They finish the edge and seam the fabric at the same time. The stitch you use depends on the type of serger you have and the weight and type of the fabric you are stitching. As a general rule, the more threads in the stitch, the more secure it is—and the more suitable it is for seaming. Keep in mind that lightweight fabrics benefit from fewer threads, and knit fabrics benefit from stitches that stretch.

THREE-THREAD OVERLOCK STITCH

uses: seams for woven and knit fabrics; edge-finishing

threading: one needle, two loopers

stitch adjustments: To change the width of this stitch, use either the right or left needle (the left needle makes a wider stitch, as explained on page 36.)

In an overlock stitch, the looper threads lock with the needle thread at the seamline and with each other at the fabric edge. Although the three-thread overlock stitch is the premier edge-finishing stitch, because it stretches, you can use it to seam knit fabrics. You can also use a wider overlock to seam medium-weight woven fabrics and a narrower version to seam lightweight woven fabrics—as long as you aren't sewing high-stress garment seams.

The three-thread overlock is a balanced stitch that looks the same on both sides, so it's ideal for reversible items. The upper looper thread lies on the right side, and the lower looper thread lies on the wrong side of the fabric as you stitch. The three-thread flatlock and rolled-edge stitches are usually formed by making tension adjustments to a three-thread overlock stitch (see pages 46 and 94).

FOUR-THREAD OVERLOCK STITCH

uses: seams for all fabrics, including knits; edge-finishing

threading: two needles, two loopers

stitch adjustments: For effective seaming, set stitch for balanced tension.

The four-thread overlock stitch resembles the three-thread overlock stitch, except it has a second row of needle stitches to the right of the first row of needle stitches. The second row adds strength and durability, making this a good stitch for seaming all types of fabrics. Both needle threads interlock with both looper threads. (The four-thread overlock is sometimes referred to as the three-thread safety overlock stitch.)

FOUR-THREAD SAFETY STITCH

uses: seams for woven fabrics; edge-finishing

threading: two needles and two loopers (upper or lower plus chain-stitch looper)

stitch adjustments: Set the machine for the chain stitch and overedge stitches.

The four-thread safety stitch is a combination of two stitches: the chain stitch (on the seamline) and the two-thread overedge stitch. These two stitches do not interlock with each other. The chain stitch provides a strong, nonstretchy seaming stitch. The overedge adds the edge-finishing touch. Together, they make a very strong construction and finishing stitch. (Check your owner's manual for the correct setup for your machine.)

FOUR-THREAD MOCK SAFETY STITCH

uses: seams in low-stress areas; edge-finishing

threading: two needles and two loopers

stitch adjustments: Check your owner's manual for setup instructions for this somewhat uncommon stitch.

Depending on your serger, you can use the four-thread mock safety stitch as an alternative to the four-thread overlock (check your owner's manual to be sure). The four-thread mock safety is less common than the overlock. Like the four-thread overlock stitch, two loopers form an overedge stitch. The locations of the two needle threads are different, however. The left-needle stitches look like a chain stitch from the right side, but they interlace with the lower looper thread (not the chain looper) on the wrong side.

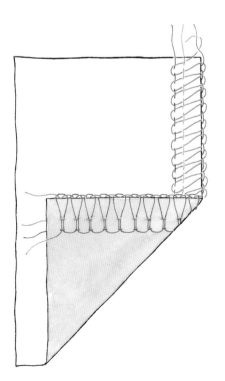

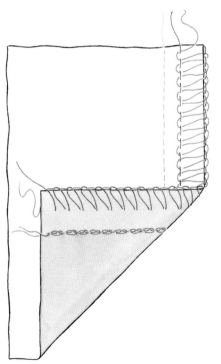

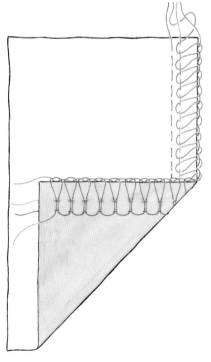

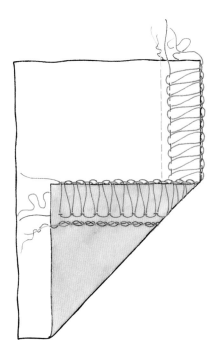

FIVE-THREAD SAFETY STITCH

uses: seams; edge-finishing in one pass
threading: two needles and three loopers
stitch adjustment: Set machine for chain stitch and three-thread overlock stitch.

The five-thread safety stitch is the strongest and most stable serger stitch, although it is only available on sergers with a five-thread capacity. The stitch itself consists of a two-thread chain-stitch seam combined with a three-thread over-lock edge finish. You can use this strong stitch to seam any woven fabric.

FIVE-THREAD+ STITCHES

Top-of-the-line sergers can create an array of decorative stitches that use more than five threads. These machines serge all of the other types of stitches, too, but they offer more decorative options. The various stitches require specific tension adjustments, and the loopers are threaded with more than one thread. The effects are created with twin and triple needles and the combinations of decorative threads. Check your owner's manual to learn what stitches are possible on your machine and for instructions as to how to set them up.

TIP

The more threads a stitch contains, the more secure it is—but the more bulk it has, too. Choose the effect you need.

COVER STITCH

This stitch, often found on knit ready-to-wear garments, features two or three parallel rows of straight stitching on one side of the fabric and, on the other side, interlocking looper threads that resemble a chain. Either side of the stitch can be used on the right side of the fabric for functional or decorative serging. The cover stitch is possible only on some five-thread sergers and on cover-stitch-only machines. It requires a special throat plate or presser foot or even a cover stitch attachment. (See pages 93–94.)

THREE-THREAD COVER STITCH

uses: hemming (especially knits); attaching elastic; decorative stitching

threading: two needles and one looper

stitch adjustment: Disengage the upper cutting knife; install specialized throat plates and/or presser feet if needed; refer to your owner's manual.

The cover stitch features parallel rows of straight stitching on the right side of the fabric and interlocking looper threads on the wrong side. Either side of the stitch can be used on the right side of the fabric. The position of the needles determines the distance between the rows of straight stitches. Standard widths are 1/8″ and 1/4″ (3 mm and 6 mm), depending on which needles you use. The needles stitch the straight rows, and the looper stitches the chain on the reverse side of the fabric.

FOUR-THREAD COVER STITCH

uses: hemming, especially knits; attaching elastic; decorative stitching

threading: three needles, one looper

stitch adjustment: Disengage the upper cutting knife; install specialized throat plates and/or presser feet if needed; refer to your owner's manual.

This stitch is often used decoratively, especially on knits, because it stretches. If the fabric tunnels between the parallel rows of stitching, loosen the needle tensions. If the fabric jams when you start to serge, place a piece of scrap fabric just in front of the presser foot. Serge onto the scrap and then directly onto the fashion fabric. This stitch unravels easily, so be sure to secure the ends (see page 62–65).

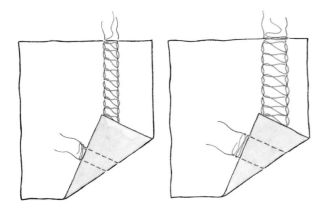 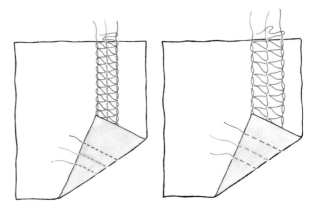

Starting to Serge

Preparation

Now that you know about the workings of your serger and the various stitch possibilities, it's time to learn the basic techniques of serger stitching. Here are some guidelines to keep in mind before you begin any project.

SAFETY FIRST

As when working with any machine, you want to be careful to protect the machine and your fingers, too. To be sure you do both, follow these few simple rules:

❖ Don't serge over pins.

❖ Don't pull the fabric as you stitch. Hold it taut, and let the machine move it through.

❖ Don't pull the fabric to remove it from the machine. If you do, you could bend the loopers. Instead, chain off, as explained on page 60, and cut the thread chain.

❖ Keep your fingers away from the needles and knives.

❖ Close the looper covers before stitching to minimize thread jams.

❖ Avoid serging very thick fabrics. The fabric might bunch up at the knives and jam the machine.

❖ Take care that trimmed fabric doesn't fall into the machine, where it could become entangled in the loopers.

❖ Always turn off the power before cleaning the machine, changing threads, and replacing knives.

TEST SAMPLE

Before you stitch your project fabric, practice on a piece of firmly woven scrap fabric. With this test sample, you can ensure that the thread tensions are balanced and the machine is threaded properly.

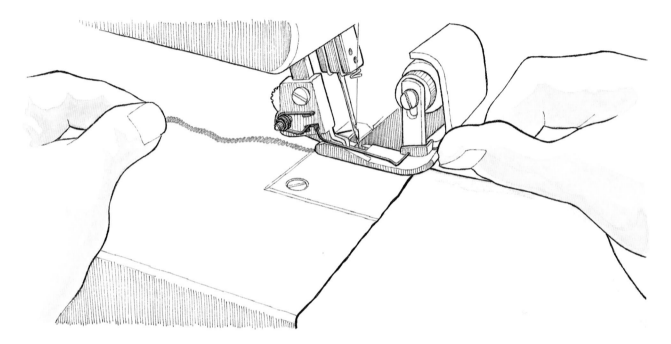

1. First, create a thread chain if there isn't one already from previous stitching. Do this by stitching without any fabric under the presser foot. Gently hold the thread tails and run the serger until the intertwined threads are between 3″ (7.6 cm) and 5″ (12.7 cm) long.

2. Position the fabric in front of the presser foot. The feed dogs will pull the fabric through. For bulky fabric, just lift the toe of the presser foot with your finger, as shown in the drawing above.

3. Guide the fabric through the serger with your hands. Position your left hand palm down to the left of the presser foot. Use the fingers of your right hand to guide the raw fabric edges an even distance from the cutting blades.

4. Start slowly. Once you see that the stitch is forming properly you can speed up. Gently guide the fabric through the machine; do not pull it. Avoid using pins. Running over a pin will damage the blades. If you need pins, position them away from the knife blades (see page 68).

5. Continue serging off the edge of the fabric and cut the thread chain. Inspect the sample. Look closely at the stitching to check the tensions. (See pages 40–43 for more information on thread tension.)

STARTING AND FINISHING

One of the most important and fundamental differences between a serger and sewing machine is that the serger can't stitch in reverse, so you can't back-tack.

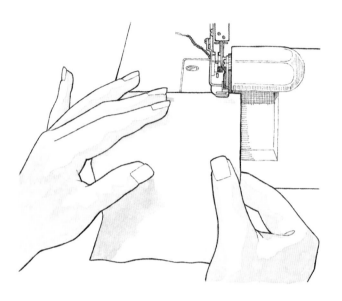

BEGINNING A SEAM

Always start with a thread chain that's at least 3″ (7.6 cm) long (see page 59). Position the fabric in front of the presser foot with the raw edge of the fabric extending to the right of the throat plate, so the knives can trim the edge. Determine how much of the edge you want trimmed away. You can trim as much as you want, but trim at least one or two thread widths to ensure a clean-cut edge under the threads.

The needle plate or bed of the serger doesn't extend beyond the needle, so there aren't marked lines to follow, as there are on a sewing machine. Some sergers have measurement guides marked on the front cover, but it's easy to watch the edge of the fabric and guide it with your hands.

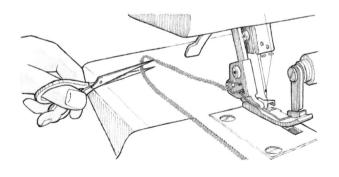

FINISHING A SEAM

Continue stitching beyond the end of the fabric to form a thread chain that is at least 6″ (15.2 cm) long. Cut the thread chain in half, leaving several inches (centimeters) attached to the machine. This process is called "chaining off."

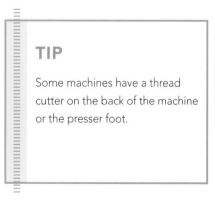

TIP

Some machines have a thread cutter on the back of the machine or the presser foot.

STITCHING AND TRIMMING FABRIC

Another important difference between a serger and sewing machine is that when you stitch with a serger, the edge of the fabric is cut off and gone forever. So, it's essential to know where the stitching line forms and where to align the fabric edge—to be sure you don't cut away too little or too much fabric.

CUTTING THE FABRIC EDGE

Position the fabric so the knives at least skim the edge of the fabric. Trimming at least 1/8″ to 3/8″ (3 mm to 1 cm) from the edge of the fabric makes a straight, neat edge. The amount you cut off depends on the desired width of the seam allowance. Follow this simple formula:

(Actual seam allowance on fabric) – (stitch width) = amount of fabric to cut away

Example:

(5/8″ [1.6 cm]-wide seam allowance) – (3/8″ [1 cm]-wide 3-thread overlock stitch) = 1/4″ (6 mm) to trim away

Example:

(1/4″ [6 mm]-wide seam allowance) – (1/4″ [6 mm]-wide 2-thread overedge stitch) = < 1/4″ (6 mm) to trim away (Just skim the edge of the fabric with the knife blades.)

SERGING ON THE STITCHING LINE

The leftmost needle stitches the seam and determines the width of the seam allowance. It is difficult to watch the knives, nee-

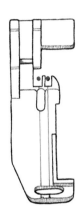

dles, and edge of the fabric at the same time. To make it easier to follow the stitching line, mark the actual stitching line on the presser foot with a permanent pen. If there are two needles, mark two stitching lines on the presser foot.

If you find it easier to guide the cut edge of the fabric, you can mark measurements on the knife guard or looper cover. Or you can purchase a measurement decal for the front of your machine. Many sergers already have the increments marked.

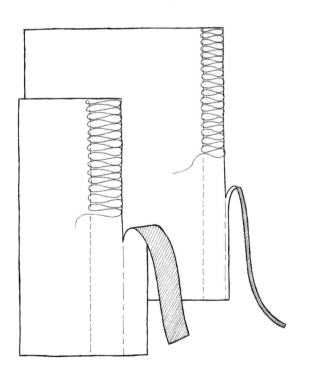

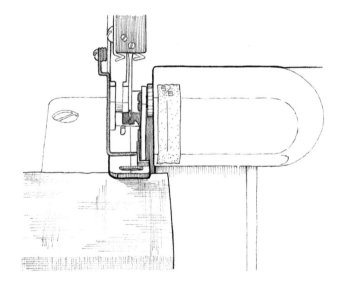

SECURING THREAD TAILS BY MACHINE

In many cases, you don't need to secure the thread tails. The beginning and end of the stitching is often enclosed within another seam or finishing detail, such as a waistband, hem, cuff, or collar. If the thread ends are dangling, however, there are several ways to secure and conceal them.

SECURING THREAD TAILS AT THE BEGINNING OF STITCHING

With a little practice, this method is easier, quicker, and even stronger than securing the thread tails by hand (see page 64).

1. Serge the first two or three stitches of the seam, about 1/4″ (6 mm).

2. Raise the presser foot, but leave the needle(s) in the fabric. Gently smooth and stretch out the thread chain and bring it around in front of the needle and under the presser foot.

3. Make sure that the stitched portion of the seam remains flat. Lower the presser foot and continue serging, stitching directly over the thread chain for at least 1″ (2.5 cm). Cut away the remaining thread chain by moving it to the right so the knife trims it.

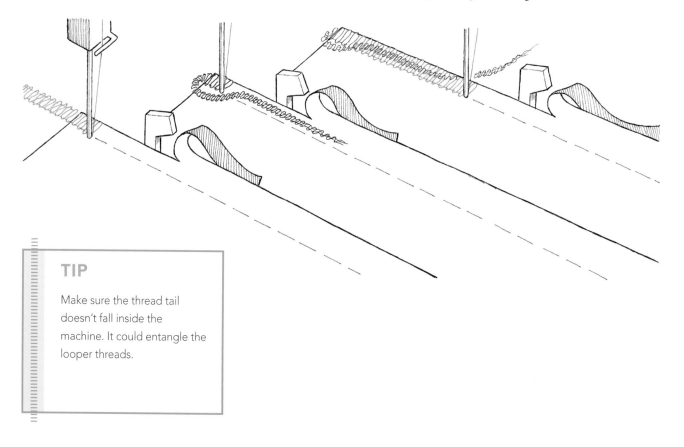

TIP

Make sure the thread tail doesn't fall inside the machine. It could entangle the looper threads.

SECURE THREAD TAILS AT THE END OF STITCHING

1. Serge two or three stitches off the end of the fabric. Carefully slip the stitches off the stitch finger (see box at right).

2. Raise the presser foot. Turn the fabric over and bring it around and in front of the presser foot.

3. Lower the presser foot and stitch 1″ to 2″ (2.5 to 5.1 cm) over the last few stitches at an angle to lock them securely. Do not cut the stitches already in place. Serge off the edge of the fabric and trim away the thread tail.

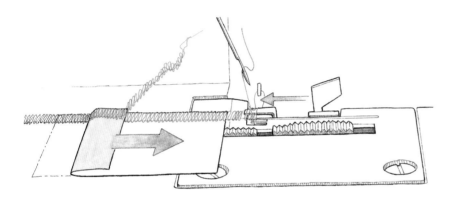

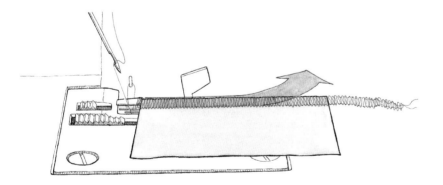

CLEARING THREAD FROM THE STITCH FINGER

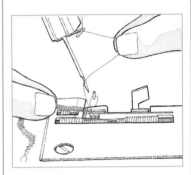

Lift the presser foot and raise the needles as high as possible. Pull the threads slightly between the needles and the last tension guide to create some slack. Gently pull the thread chain toward the back of the machine, sliding the stitches off the stitch finger. Before you resume stitching, remove the extra thread slack by pulling it through to the thread spool or above the tension control.

SECURING THREAD TAILS BY HAND

In some cases, you may need to secure thread tails after you've removed the project from the serger. If you do, securing is easy and fast to do by hand. There are three ways to do it.

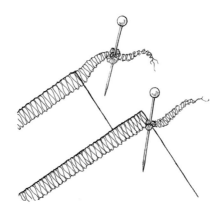

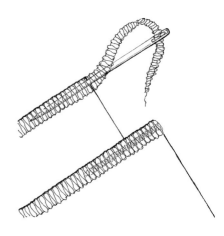

SECURING THREADS WITH SEAM SEALANT

Just a dab of seam sealant on the threads, near the fabric edge, will prevent unraveling. Trim the thread chain after the sealant is dry. Apply seam sealant only to the thread, not the fabric. If the sealant container doesn't have a fine tip, a pin makes a good applicator.

SECURE THREADS WITH KNOTTING

Tie the thread chain in a knot near the edge of the fabric. To get the knot as close as possible to the fabric edge, insert a straight pin into the center of the knot. Use the pin to move the knot down the thread close to the fabric edge, then pull the thread to tighten. For added security, apply seam sealant. Trim the thread ends.

SECURE THREADS BY CONCEALING ENDS

Thread the chain onto a blunt tapestry needle and insert the needle under the stitches for about 2″ to 3″ (5.1 cm to 7.6 cm). Smooth out the loops of the chain and trim the thread ends to an even length for easier threading.

TIP

Rubbing alcohol removes sealant from fabric, but test it on a seam allowance first to make sure it doesn't cause discoloration.

REMOVING SERGER STITCHES

The easiest way to remove serger stitches is to trim away the serged edge with scissors or a rotary cutter—or to re-serge the edge to the left of the existing stitches. If you don't have sufficient seam allowance left to cut away the stitches, pull them out with a seam ripper or your fingers. Here's how to undo basic serger stitches.

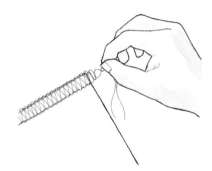

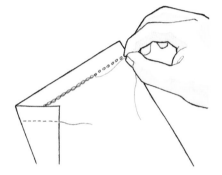

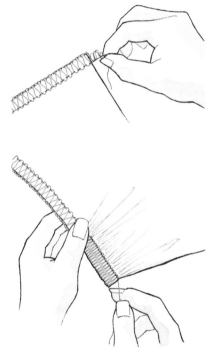

removing two-thread overedge stitches: Gently pull the needle and looper threads together, and the stitches will pull right out.

removing cover stitches: Clip the last few stitches formed by the needle threads from the right side of the fabric. Turn the fabric over and gently pull the looper thread to unravel the entire stitch.

removing flatlock stitches: Pull the lower looper thread or undo each stitch, one at a time, with a straight pin.

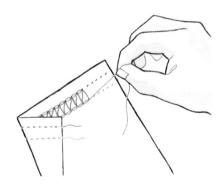

removing two-thread chain stitches: This stitch is so easy to pull out that you can use it as a basting stitch (see page 46). Cut the chain close to the end of the stitching. Working with a straight pin, separate the threads and pull the looper thread. The chain stitch will unravel.

removing three- or four-thread overlock stitches: Smooth out the chain and find the shortest thread(s), which will be the needle thread(s). Gently pull them, sliding the fabric so it gathers along the threads. Pull them right through all the stitches and off the fabric. Then pull the looper threads free in long, continuous strands.

Stitching Techniques

EDGE-FINISHING CONVENTIONAL SEAMS

Your serger won't replace your sewing machine, but it can take on a lot of jobs. You only need to learn a few simple techniques to get the most from your serger. Here's how to handle everything—from basic seam finishing to serging circles.

Edge-finishing is done on fabric edges, including the seam allowances of conventionally sewn seams. To create a professional-looking finish on almost any fabric edge, simply run the cut edge of the fabric through the serger. (See pages 44–55 for descriptions of individual serger stitches to choose one that's suitable for your fabric.)

Conventional seams are more suitable than serged seams when the garment requires wide seam allowances—either because the fabric is heavyweight or ravels extensively or because the garment may call for future alterations. There are three ways to serge-finish conventionally sewn seams:

1. Straight-stitch the seam and press it flat as sewn, as shown in drawing **A**. Overlock or overedge the seam allowances together, 1/8″ to 1/4″ (3 mm to 6 mm) from the stitching line. This type of seam is most suitable for lightweight fabrics.

2. Straight-stitch the seam, then press the seam allowances open. Overlock or overedge the seam allowances separately. (Opt for this method if you might want to alter the garment at a later date.)

3. Overlock the fabric edges as soon as you transfer the pattern markings and remove the patterns. Use tailor's tacks or fabric markers, not clips or notches, so you don't serge away the markings. Then machine-stitch as usual.

A.

B.

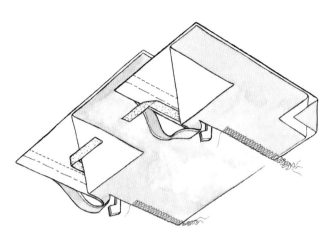

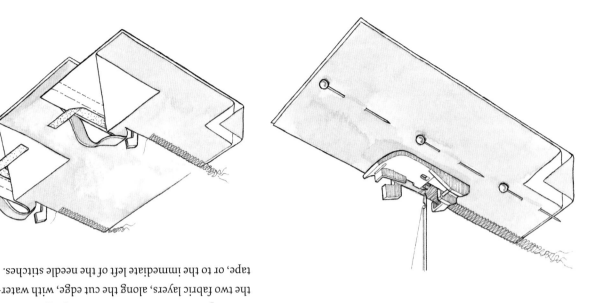

BASTING

Even though serging speeds up your sewing, sometimes you'll need to take the time to baste your seams together before you serge. Basting allows you to secure the fabric layers together before you cut away the seam allowance.

BASTING OPTIONS

There are several basting methods that work well, including chain-stitch basting, pin basting, hand basting, and basting with tape or glue. Select a method that offers enough control for your particular fabric type. You also want to be sure the basting stitches will be easy to remove when you no longer need them.

chain-stitch basting: This stitch is easy to rip out (see page 65). Just remember that if you are basting away from the fabric edge, you need to disengage the knives. Set the serger for the chain stitch (check your owner's manual for specific instructions for your machine).

fabric basting glue: Check that the glue doesn't change the hand of the fabric. Apply the glue sparingly—and within the seam allowance whenever possible.

hand basting: If you are really concerned about slippage because of your fabric type, simply hand-sew the fabric layers together with long, loose running stitches.

pin basting: Position the pins to the left of and parallel to the presser foot, well away from the knives, so you can pull them out easily. Choose pins with large, colored heads that are easy to see.

basting tape: Some tapes leave a sticky residue and shouldn't be stitched through; some can be stitched through; and some are water-soluble. Be sure to test any tape on a fabric scrap first. If the tape shouldn't be stitched through, position it between the two fabric layers, along the cut edge, with water-soluble tape, or to the immediate left of the needle stitches.

WHEN TO BASTE

- when you want to check the fit of a garment before seaming
- when you're handling very slippery fabrics
- when matching a print or pattern is important
- when the project contains curved or intricate seams

THE BASIC SERGER SEAM

You can use several different serger stitches for seaming (see pages 46–55). Choosing the right stitch depends on how strong the seam needs to be, the type and weight of the fabric, and the elasticity (or stretch) of the fabric.

SEAM STITCH SELECTION

❖ Both three- and four-thread overlock stitches are suitable for some types of seaming. The three-thread seam has more elasticity and is best suited to knit fabrics. A four-thread overlock stitch is more stable and stronger, suitable for wovens. Remember that in a four-thread stitch the left needle stitches the seamline.

❖ The four-thread and five-thread safety overlock stitches include the chain stitch. The chain stitch forms the seamline, and either a two-thread overedge or three-thread overlock stitch adds security. The chain stitch can be used for seaming, as long as you secure the thread ends so it doesn't come undone.

SERGING A SEAM

After you've selected your stitch, you're ready to make the serged seam. Just follow these five steps to ensure a perfectly stitched seam:

plan: Because the serger cuts the fabric, it is important to plan how wide to cut the seam allowance (see page 61) and how wide a stitch to choose.

mark: Do not mark with fabric notches or snips cut into the seam allowance; they will be trimmed away during serging. Draw all the markings directly on the fabric with chalk or a fabric-marking pen. Test both on the fabric first.

pin: If you baste with pins, position them as described on page 68. Check that the pins don't mar the fabric or leave holes that will be visible in the finished item.

stitch and cut: Begin stitching slowly, either following the seamline marks on the presser foot or guiding the fabric edge along the mark on the front of the machine (see page 61). If your machine isn't marked, you can add a strip of tape with markings. As you gain confidence, speed up.

press: Press the serged seam flat. Then open the fabric and press the seam allowances to one side.

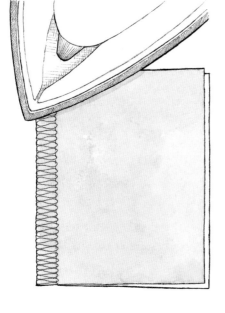
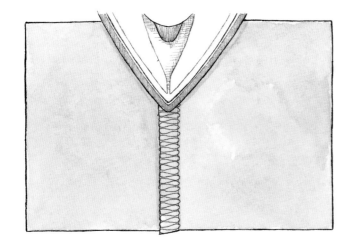

PREVENTING PUCKERED OR STRETCHED FABRIC

One of the joys of sewing with a serger is the ability to prevent, or at least minimize, puckered or stretched seams. The key is the differential feed feature, a standard item on most new machines (see page 37). If your machine doesn't have differential feed, you can make other adjustments and manually help feed the fabric. Typically, puckered seams can be a problem with silky fabrics, and stretching can be a problem with knits.

MACHINE ADJUSTMENTS

You can adjust your serger to minimize puckering or stretching as you stitch.

differential feed: Adjust the differential feed, as explained on page 37, to a negative setting to minimize puckering and to a positive setting to minimize stretching.

needle tensions: Loosen the needle tensions if there are puckers along the seamline.

presser foot pressure: The presser foot controls how much pressure is exerted on the fabric (see page xx). Decrease the pressure to minimize stretching. Increase the pressure to minimize puckering.

stitch length: To minimize puckering, shorten the stitch length slightly. To minimize stretching, lengthen the stitch.

manual fabric feed: If your machine doesn't have a differential feed function, help control the movement of the fabric under the presser foot, in one of two ways:

❖ Ease the fabric to minimize stretching. Feed the fabric to the presser foot so it enters the stitch more quickly, by gently holding the fabric in front of the presser foot. You can also hold the fabric against the back of the presser foot with your other hand to slow its exit from the stitch, as shown in the drawing below at left.

❖ Hold the fabric taut in front of and behind the presser foot to minimize puckering, as shown in the drawing below at right. Don't pull the fabric, just hold it and sew at a slow, even speed.

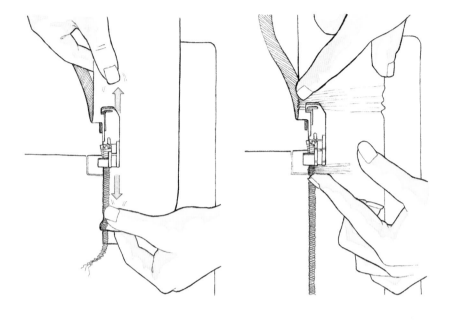

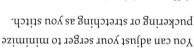

SERGING CORNERS

Serging both inside and outside corners requires special techniques. It's difficult to see a corner's exact pivot point under the serger's long presser foot. Also, it's difficult to pivot fabric on a serger.

INSIDE CORNERS

Inside corners are easier to serge than outside corners. By manipulating the fabric, you can almost treat the inside corners as if they were a straight seam.

If you plan to trim the seam allowance, cut it from both edges of the corner with scissors for about 2″ (5.1 cm) before you start serging. If you are just skimming the edge of the fabric, don't cut the corner with scissors first.

Serge the first side until the knife is about 1/2″ (1.3 cm) from the adjacent corner. Leave the needle in the fabric.

Raise the presser foot and pull the fabric to open the corner into a straight edge. The fabric forms V-shaped folds to the left of the presser foot. Lower the presser foot and continue serging. The needle will barely enter the fabric at the corner.

TIP

Serge the edges of a slit just as you would an inside corner. Gently open the slit by folding one or more tucks so that they extend away from the top of the slit opening.

OUTSIDE CORNERS

You have two options for serging outside corners. You can serge the sides separately or in one pass.

serging each side separately: Serge one side and chain off. Gently pivot the fabric, pulling the thread chain to guide the corner back under the foot. Serge the next side, trimming the thread chain as you stitch.

SERGING SHARP CORNERS

For sharp corners, angle the last three or four stitches inward about 1/8" (3 mm). As you begin stitching the next corner, stitch the first three or four stitches about 1/8" (3 mm) inside the stitching line. Then continue along the stitching line.

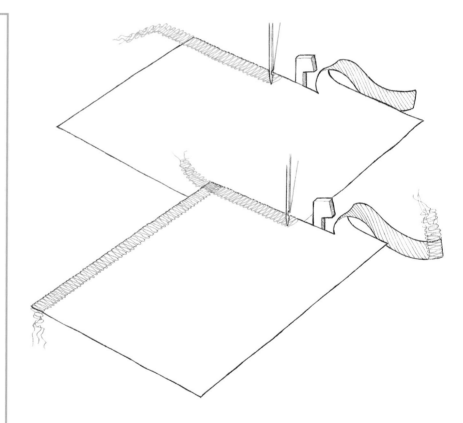

serging in one pass: If you're trimming a seam allowance, cut the seam allowance from the second edge of the corner with scissors for about 2″ (5.1 cm), as shown in the drawing. If you are just skimming the edge of the fabric, follow the instructions below without cutting away the corner first.

Serge one stitch beyond the corner of the fabric. Raise the needle and the presser foot. Clear the stitch finger (see page 63).

Pivot the fabric and lower the needle so it enters the fabric on the stitching line. The edge of the fabric should align with the knife. Lower the presser foot and continue serging. If there is a small loop of thread at the corner, gently pull the needle thread(s) above the appropriate tension dial(s) before you resume stitching.

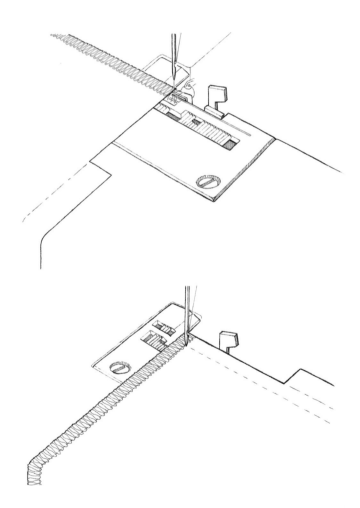

TIP

If you don't need perfectly square corners, round the corners into gentle curves before starting to stitch.

SERGING CURVES

Serging curves calls for slow, steady stitching and a careful eye on the point where the knives cut the fabric. It is easier to serge a gentle curve than a tight one.

TIPS FOR SERGING AROUND CURVES

If your machine has differential feed, increase the setting slightly to minimize stretching the fabric edge. It is easier to serge a curved area if you cut away all but 1/8″ (3 mm) of the seam allowance. A narrower stitch width also helps keep your stitching even around tight curves. Watch the knives rather than the needles to guide the fabric edge accurately.

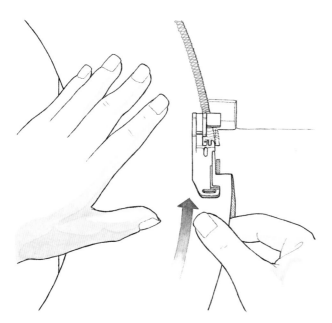

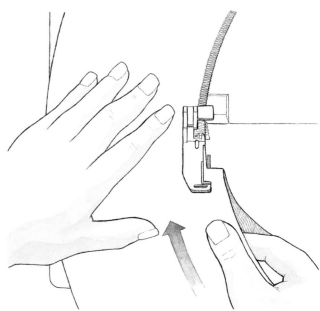

OUTSIDE CURVES

Stitch slowly, continually shifting the fabric edge slightly toward the right in front of the presser foot. This shifting will keep the stitching line straight. If the curve is tight, stop periodically, lift the presser foot, and shift the fabric very slightly. Then lower the presser foot and resume stitching.

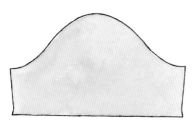

INSIDE CURVES

Stitch slowly and shift the fabric edge as for an outside curve, but to the left instead of the right. Take care not to stretch the fabric.

JOINING OPPOSING CURVES

When you serge an armhole or princess seam, you're serging an outside curve to an inside curve. Serge for about 1″ (2.5 cm), stop, and then lift the presser foot slightly so the fabric relaxes. Lower the presser foot and repeat. Continue in this way to complete the entire seam or edge finish.

SERGING CIRCULAR EDGES

There are two ways to serge around a circular item, such as a hem or an appliqué. You can use these same techniques any time that you want to begin and end your stitching at the same point.

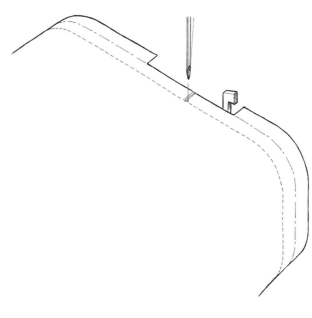

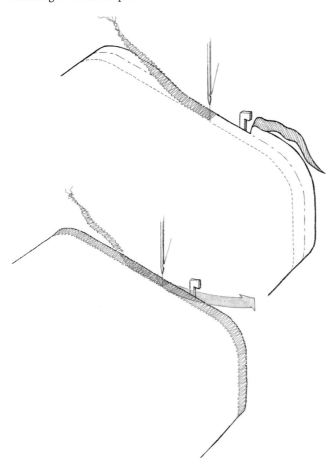

OVERLAPPING THE STITCHES

This method is the quickest way to overlap stitches, but is also the most visible. Angle the beginning stitches so that you have fabric to trim away when you arrive back at the beginning. Simply serge around the edge and over the beginning stitches. Overlap the stitches by 1/2″ to 1″ (1.3 to 2.5 cm), without trimming them. Angle the stitching off the fabric. Trim the chain and secure it. Depending on the texture of the thread, you may be able to conceal the overlapping stitches.

ABUTTING THE STITCHES

This method creates the cleanest appearance, but you need adequate seam allowance to work with for a smooth start and finish. Cut a 2″ (5.1 cm)-long section of the seam allowance away at the point where you want the stitching to begin and end. The depth of the cut-out section should equal the width of the fabric that will be trimmed away.

Begin and end the stitching within the pretrimmed section. To start, raise the needle and presser foot. Clear the stitch finger (see page 63) and pull the threads to the back and left of the presser foot. Position the fabric with the knife at the front of the cut-away area. Lower the presser foot and begin stitching, allowing the serger to trim the remaining seam allowance. When you reach the beginning stitches, raise the presser foot and clear the stitch finger. Pull the fabric away from the needle and knife. Continue serging to create a thread chain. Cut the chain and secure the ends.

Construction Techniques

You'll be surprised to learn how many essential construction steps you can accomplish with the serger. Some garments can be sewn entirely on the serger, in record time and with professional-looking results! Here are a few techniques you can perform with your serger.

GATHERING

With a serger, you can gather fabric in one step, and much more quickly than with the sewing machine. It's especially easy when you work with the differential feed feature (see page 37) and/or a shirring presser foot.

GATHERING GUIDELINES

- Always test your settings on scrap fabric first.

- Usually, the longer the stitch setting, the more the fabric will gather.

- Set the serger to a three- or four-thread overlock stitch.

- Soft, lightweight fabrics gather better than heavy, stiff fabrics.

- Experiment with machine settings to get the right amount of gathering (see page 78).

- Don't try to gather fabric that ravels excessively.

- Don't try to gather pieces that need a wider than normal seam allowance.

- The fabric type, weight, and grain affect the fullness of the gathers.

TIP

Serger-gathering is an ideal technique for home décor projects with long lengths of ruffles.

GATHERING A SINGLE LAYER WITHOUT DIFFERENTIAL FEED

Set the serger for the widest possible three- or four-thread overlock stitch and tighten the needle tension to nearly the maximum setting. Serge along the fabric edge and the fabric will gather up automatically.

To produce more gathers, lengthen the stitch, decrease the presser foot pressure, and/ or pull the needle thread after serging to create more gathers on the serged fabric.

To produce fewer, softer gathers, lightly press the needle thread to the machine above the tension dial as you stitch—this method also works to ease fabric slightly.

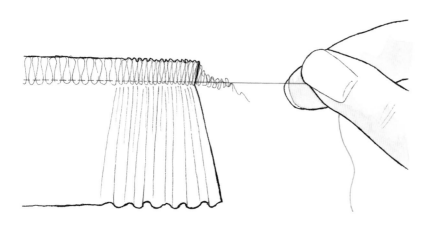

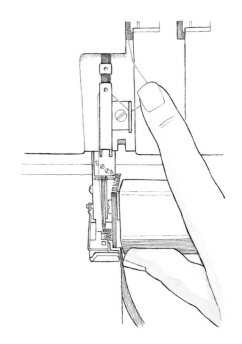

GATHERING A SINGLE LAYER WITH DIFFERENTIAL FEED

Set the serger for a three- or four-thread overlock stitch with longer-than-usual stitch length. Adjust the differential feed to its highest setting. Place the fabric edge in front of the presser foot and serge, allowing the fabric to feed freely through the machine.

For more gathers, lengthen the stitch, and increase the needle thread tension. For fewer gathers, shorten the stitch length, and reduce the differential feed setting.

GATHERING ONE LAYER TO ANOTHER

A serger also makes it easy to gather or ease a length of fabric while at the same time attaching it to a shorter length of fabric. Install the shirring foot and set the differential feed to the highest setting. Set the machine to a three- or four-thread overlock stitch. Gathering reduces the longer piece to about half its original length, so be sure to cut it so it's twice the length of the shorter piece.

The shirring foot gathers the lower layer of the fabric while the serger sews the two layers together, in one quick step. Position the fabrics with right sides together, with the longer fabric on the bottom and the shorter piece on top. Stitch slowly.

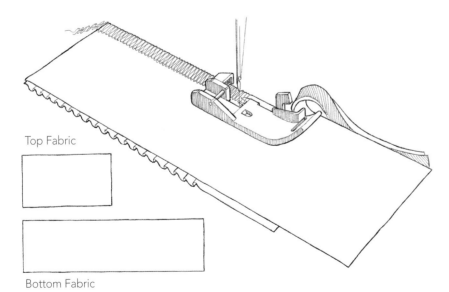

Top Fabric

Bottom Fabric

SPECIALTY SEAMS

Now that you've learned the basic seaming stitches, you can experiment with combining serger and sewing machine stitches to create new seam types. These seams can be extra-strong, reversible, or simply decorative.

Choosing the best seam depends on the type and weight of your fabric and the desired look. A few specialty seams are described below. (See pages 96–101 for flatlocking seams and page 81 for rolled-edge seams.)

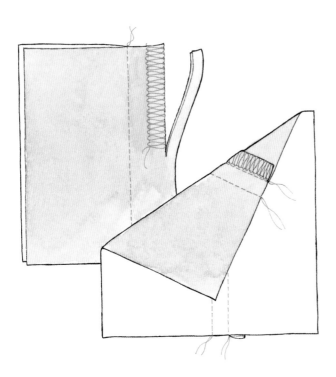

FLAT-FELL SEAM

The flat-fell seam is strong and durable and is often used on denim and other heavyweight fabrics. With right sides together, straight-stitch the seam with a 5/8" (1.6 cm) seam allowance, on the sewing machine or with a chain serger stitch. With a three-thread overlock stitch, serge the seam allowances together, letting the knives skim the edges.

Press the seam allowances to one side. Working on the right side of the fabric, topstitch with the sewing machine, close to the seam, and then topstitch again 1/4" (6 mm) away, catching the seam allowance in the stitch, as shown in the drawing.

FRENCH SEAM

A French seam is ideal for sewing sheer, lightweight fabrics. Start with 5/8" (1.6 cm) seam allowances. With wrong sides together and the serger set for a narrow three-thread overlock stitch, serge the seam. Trim about 1/4" (6 mm) of the fabric edges away as you stitch.

Press the stitches flat and then press the fabric with the right sides together and the serged seam between the layers. With the sewing machine, straight-stitch close to the enclosed seam.

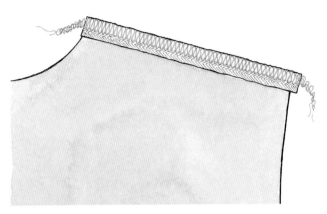

REINFORCED SEAM

To prevent a seam from stretching out of shape or raveling, reinforce it with twill tape or clear elastic. Insert the tape or elastic through the slot in the standard presser foot as you serge the seam. Or, align it with the cut edge, so it is caught in the stitching. This technique is useful for stabilizing shoulder seams, waistlines, and other horizontal seams, especially in knits.

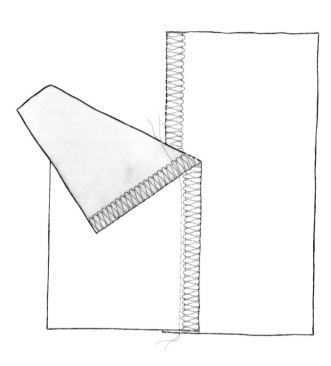

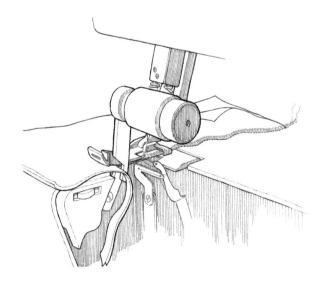

LAPPED SEAM

The lapped seam has visible stitching, which creates a casual, sporty look. You can enhance this effect by working with decorative threads.

Serge the edge of each of the two pieces to be joined with a three-thread overlock stitch. The needle should stitch directly on the seamlines. Overlap the serged edges so the stitching lines align. Glue or pin-baste them together. With the sewing machine, topstitch through both layers over the seamline.

ROLLED-EDGE SEAM

Seaming is not the primary use for a rolled-edge stitch, but it works well on sheer fabrics because it minimizes visible seam allowances. Simply serge the seam with the right sides of the fabric together, trimming the seam allowances as you serge.

APPLYING ELASTIC

Applying elastic with the serger is a straightforward process, so you can create professional-looking sportswear very quickly and easily. Attach the elastic directly to the fabric or insert it in a serged casing.

DIRECT APPLICATION

Clear elastic is most suitable for direct application because it stretches and recovers well. Another advantage is that if you nick it with the knife, it won't tear apart. Choose direct application when you want to form a ruffle at the wrist or ankle, gather the waist, or finish bathing suit or lingerie leg openings. This method is much easier to work on a straight edge, before the edge is seamed into a circle. So leave one side seam unstitched, attach the elastic, and then stitch the garment opening closed.

1. Cut a length of elastic to fit snugly around the desired body location, adding 1″ (2.5 cm) for seam allowance. Divide the elastic into quarters and mark. Divide the fabric into quarters at the elastic's placement location and mark.

2. Place the elastic in front of the presser foot so the edge of the elastic clears the knife. Serge two or three stitches to secure the elastic. Stop stitching with the needle down. Lift the presser foot and slip the fabric, wrong side up, under the elastic. Leave about 1/8″ (3 mm) of fabric extending beyond the elastic so the knife will trim it.

3. Stitch slowly with a three-thread overlock stitch and a slightly longer stitch length. Stretch the elastic and match the elastic and fabric markings as you serge. If you need to, stop with the needle down and raise the presser foot to stretch the elastic.

4. Leave the elastic exposed on the inside of the garment or fold it under so it's wrapped by fabric. Topstitch it in place with a straight sewing machine stitch or a serger chain stitch. If the elastic stretches out of shape, hold an iron over it and apply bursts of steam.

TIP

You can also directly apply elastic with an elastic presser foot. This foot has a slot to slide the elastic through. The stitches form over the elastic as it is fed through the foot.

ELASTIC IN A CASING

There are several ways to form an elasticized casing. Some involve working with both the sewing machine and the serger. If the casing is circular, sew the side seams first, before applying the elastic.

inserting the elastic through an opening in the topstitching: Edge-finish the top edge of the casing with any overedge stitch. Fold the fabric to the wrong side the desired amount (width of elastic + about 1″ [2.5 cm]). Topstitch the serged edge to the fabric with a straight sewing machine stitch, or use a serger chain stitch with the knives deactivated. Stop 1″ to 2″ (2.5 to 5.1 cm) before you get back to the beginning of the seam.

Work with a safety pin to thread the elastic through the casing. Sew the ends of the elastic together by machine. Then close the stitching by completing the topstitching.

encasing the elastic during stitching with a serged cover stitch: You don't need to edge-finish the top fabric edge; the cover stitch finishes it during the final step. Fold the fabric to the wrong side, to the width of the elastic plus about 1/4″ (6 mm), then press. Cut the elastic, overlap the ends, and stitch them together with the cover stitch. Place the elastic under the fabric fold, aligning it against the crease.

Set the serger to the cover stitch and serge, stretching the elastic so the fabric is flat your stitch. Don't catch the elastic in the stitching.

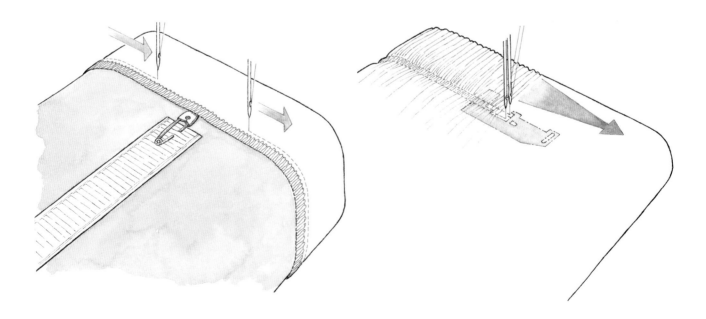

HEMMING

The serger offers many hemming options, most of which can be done in much less time than hemming with the sewing machine or by hand. Quick hemming is most certainly one of the best aspects of serger ownership!

EDGE-FINISHED HEMS

An edge-finished hem can be made with a variety of stitches, but narrow stitches look the best. Edge-finished hems are appropriate for woven and knit fabrics of any weight. They're helpful for finishing sheer fabrics and also for finishing heavier fabrics that are difficult to ease into a rolled edge.

Many decorative narrow hems require setting the serger up for a two-thread rolled-edge stitch (see page 47). If you don't want, or need, the fabric edge to roll to the wrong side, try serging just the edge for a quick and easy hem finish.

overlocked cut edge: Set the serger for a narrow, three-thread overlock stitch (see page 50). Then simply serge along the cut edge, with or without decorative thread in the upper looper.

thread-wrapped cut edge: Set the serger for a two-thread overedge stitch (see page 45). You can finesse the width by using the right needle for a narrow stitch or the left needle for a wider stitch. Because there are only two threads, this overedge stitch is one of the least bulky stitches, making it perfect for hemming sheer and lightweight fabrics. The finished effect looks just like a rolled edge, with a dense edging of thread, and is often used to duplicate the look of a rolled edge on medium- to heavyweight fabrics.

HEM OR EDGE FINISH?

Hemming involves folding a predetermined fabric allowance to the inside to adjust for a project's desired length. For a traditional hem, which is appropriate for nearly all types and weights of fabrics, you need to clean-finish the raw edge of the fabric and then anchor the finished edge to the inside of the project. Edge-finishing involves simply serging the fabric edge. There are several novelty variations on this type of finish, as explained on pages 88–89 and page 106. Edge finishes are usually worked on light- to medium-weight fabrics.

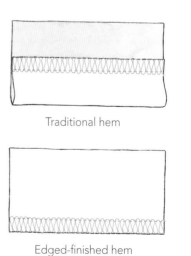

Traditional hem

Edged-finished hem

FOLDED HEMS

A folded hem is often made with a combination of serger stitches and hand or sewing machine stitches.

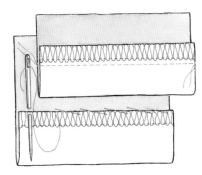

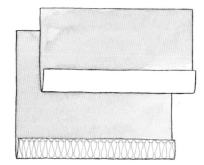

hem depth greater than 5/8" (1.6 cm): Determine the desired depth of the hem allowance and then overlock the raw edge with a three-thread overlock stitch. Fold the hem allowance to the wrong side. Then machine-topstitch it in place, sew it by hand, or press on a fusible product to secure it.

hem depth less than 5/8" (1.6 cm): For fine or loosely woven fabrics, fold and press under the bottom edge 1/4" to 3/8" (6 mm to 1 cm). Overlock-stitch over the folded fabric to give the hem edge a little more weight.

BLINDSTITCHING TIPS

- Choose this hem type for medium-weight fabrics only.

- Set the serger for a three-thread overlock stitch with a long stitch length. Install the needle in the right needle position.

- Make a test sample on scrap fabric and check the stitch. If too much thread is visible on the right side of the fabric, lengthen the stitch and adjust the stitch width as desired.

- Install a blind-hem presser foot, if you have one—it has a bar that protects the fabric from the knife.

- Hem the fabric flat, before sewing one of the side seams, if possible.

BLINDSTITCHED HEMS

The blindstitched hem made on the serger is much like the one made on a sewing machine. The only difference is that the serged version overcasts the bottom edge and secures the hem allowance in one step. It's a good hem treatment for both woven and knit fabrics.

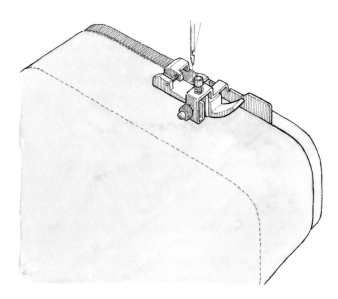

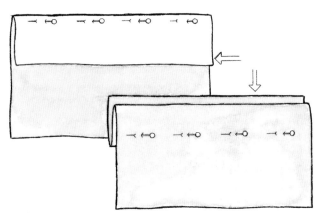

1. Mark the hemline on the right side of the project. Fold the hem allowance under along the marking. Pin close to the fold.

2. Fold the hem allowance again so that the cut edge of the hem extends about 1/4″ (6 mm) beyond the fold, as shown in the drawing.

3. Pin the layers carefully. Position the fold of the fabric next to the bar (and/or under the groove) of the presser foot. Serge slowly, allowing the needle to penetrate the fabric fold and the knife to skim the raw edge as the loopers overcast it. Remove the pins as you stitch. Unfold the hem and press it flat.

INSERTING A ZIPPER

You might not want to insert all types of zipper with your serger—but if you have an exposed zipper, you certainly can. The garment or item must have a seam, collar, or facing that is perpendicular to the zipper at each end. The serger can't navigate around the pull tab or bottom stop. Instead, you'll cut off the ends and use other construction details to keep the zipper pull from falling off.

SERGING THE ZIPPER IN PLACE

1. Mark the seamline on the right side of both fabric pieces. Open the zipper and pin the zipper tape on the right side of one fabric piece, aligning the teeth directly over the seamline. The pull tab and end stop should extend beyond the edges of the fabric, as shown in the drawing. The cut edge of the fabric should extend about 1/8″ (3 mm) beyond the edge of the zipper tape.

2. With the zipper teeth to the left of the needle, serge the zipper in place. Trim away approximately 1/8″ (3 mm) of fabric, without nicking the zipper tape.

3. Remove the piece from the serger. Fold under the zipper tape, smooth the fabric away from the zipper, and press. Topstitch close to the folded edge.

4. Repeat steps 1–3 with the second fabric piece. Lower the zipper pull tab so it doesn't extend beyond the upper fabric edge. Serge or sew any intersecting seams, collars, or facings. Cut off the bottom and top ends of the zipper with scissors. Then reinforce the zipper ends with several hand stitches across the teeth (made over the previous stitching so they are invisible).

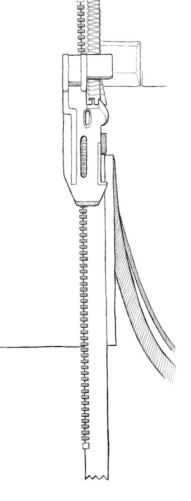

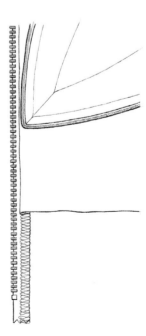

ROLLED-EDGE TECHNIQUES

The rolled-edge stitch is one of the most popular serger stitches. It creates a narrow, neat edge that is formed as the serger trims, rolls, and stitches the fabric edge in one pass. The stitch length adjustment is crucial. If the stitch length is too short, the fabric edge can be heavy and stiff. If the stitches are too long, the fabric edge can pucker. Adjust your serger as explained on pages 46–47.

ROLLED-EDGE HEMS

The standard rolled-edge stitch produces a narrow but visible hem. You can work with two threads or three, depending on how much thread you want in the hem. The two-thread rolled edge is best for lightweight, fine fabrics; the three-thread version for heavier fabrics.

When you cut the project, leave a hem allowance of between 1/8″ and 1/4″ (3 and 6 mm). Then you can trim the hem slightly as you stitch to produce a neater stitch. With the right side up, insert the fabric edge under the presser foot. Serge slowly.

To reduce puckering, turn the differential feed to a slightly lower setting, as described on page 37, or practice taut serging, described on page 70. Keep the speed of the machine even to minimize irregular or skipped stitches.

When you're working with very sheer or lightweight fabric, you'll often get a better rolled edge if you add a second layer of fabric. Press under a narrow hem allowance—about 1/2″ (1.3 cm). Serge along the folded edge. After the stitching is complete, trim away the hem allowance close to the stitching.

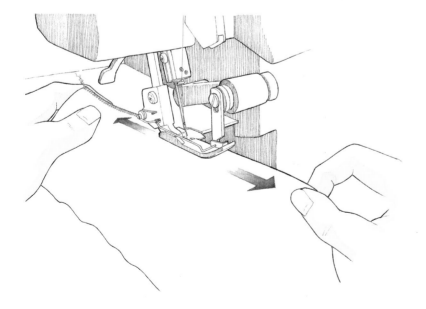

SPECIAL EFFECTS WITH ROLLED EDGES

The rolled-edge stitch lends itself to both decorative and functional finishes. Experiment to find out which effects work best on your fabric.

lettuce edge: This rippled edge can only be stitched on fabrics that have some give. Ribbing, crossgrain knits, bias-cut wovens, spandex, tricot, sweater knits, and lingerie fabrics are perfect. Set the differential feed at the negative setting. Typically, lightweight fabrics, shorter stitch length, and stretchy thread (for example, wooly nylon) create the most dramatic lettuce leaf effect. Serge along the edge of the fabric, stretching the fabric as you stitch and skimming off about 1/8″ (3 mm) of the fabric.

fishline edge: The fishline edge gives ruffles flair and fluidity. You actually incorporate nylon fishing line into a lettuce edge. Set the serger for a three-thread rolled edge. Work with 10- to 15-pound (4.5 to 6.8 kg) fishing line for fine fabrics like tulle and georgette; 25- to 40-pound (11.3 to 18.1 kg) line for heavier fabrics, like taffeta.

Leave long tails of fishing line at each end of the stitching. Place the fishing line over the front and under the back of the presser foot. Guide the fishing line between the knife and the needle and stitch directly over the line for a few inches (centimeters). Then insert the fabric with the right side up under the line. Slowly continue stitching the line to the fabric, stretching the fabric slightly.

When the stitching is complete, continue serging over the line, but off the fabric. Trim the fishing line to leave a 4″ to 5″ tail (10.2 to 12.7 cm). Smooth the stitches and gently spread the fabric over the fishing line. Thread the remaining tails under the stitching (see page 64).

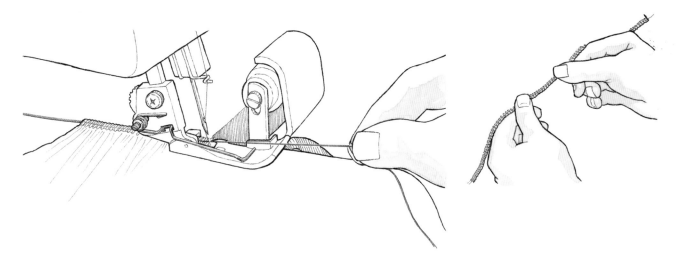

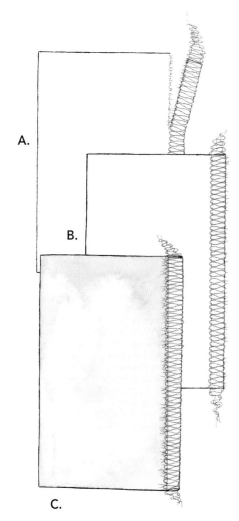

A.

B.

C.

TROUBLESHOOTING ROLLED-EDGE PROBLEMS

To solve a stitch problem, try one strategy at a time. If that remedy doesn't work, go back to the original setting and try the next possible solution. Practice serging after each attempt.

if the fabric doesn't roll: Try washing the fabric to remove any sizing. If that doesn't work, the fabric may be too thick or springy. Try working with an overedge finish instead.

if the stitches don't cover the fabric edge: Shorten the stitch length; or use a fuller thread (like wooly nylon) or multiple strands of thread in the upper looper (and loosen tension accordingly).

if the hem tears away from the fabric: If the hem detaches (**A**), lengthen the stitch; increase the cutting width; change to a smaller needle.

if threads poke out of the stitch: This problem usually occurs with fabrics that are a little stiff or heavy. If fabric fibers poke out away from the fabric, increase the amount of fabric that rolls under the stitches. Also widen the stitch (**B**). If fabric fibers poke in toward the fabric, reduce the amount of fabric that is trimmed and make the stitch narrower (**C**).

if the fabric puckers: Loosen the needle tension; set the differential feed to a lower-than-normal setting; use taut sewing (see page 70); try a smaller needle; lengthen the stitch length slightly; make sure you trim some fabric as you stitch.

if stitching is uneven: Trim a little more of the fabric edge as you serge; avoid working with textured fabrics that don't fold consistently.

COVER STITCH TECHNIQUES

If your serger can make a cover stitch, you can duplicate lots of ready-to-wear effects. On its right side, the stitch consists of two or three rows of parallel straight stitching; on its wrong side, it forms a series of loops. The cover stitch is a flexible, stretchy stitch and so it's often used on knit garments.

Some sergers have two needle positions, so you can choose between two stitch widths. The wider stitch has 5 mm to 6 mm (3/16″ to 1/4″) between the needles. The narrower stitch has 2.5 mm to 3 mm (3/32″ to 1/8″) between the needles.

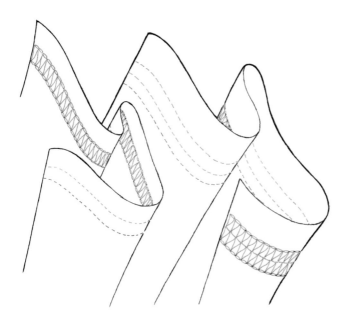

TIP

For a cover-stitch look, finish the fabric edge with a three-thread overlock stitch. Press the hem allowance to the wrong side and topstitch the right side with a twin needle.

COVER-STITCHING TIPS

- Practice on scrap fabric first, stitching through two layers. On the right side, keep the stitching rows parallel to the fabric edge. On the wrong side, the loops should cover the raw fabric edge.

- Increase the differential feed setting if the fabric is a knit and stretches.

- Steam-press a stretched seam back into shape.

- Work with medium-weight fabrics for the best-looking results.

- Loosen the needle tension to keep the fabric from tunneling between the rows of stitching.

- Secure the thread ends to avoid unraveling (see page 94).

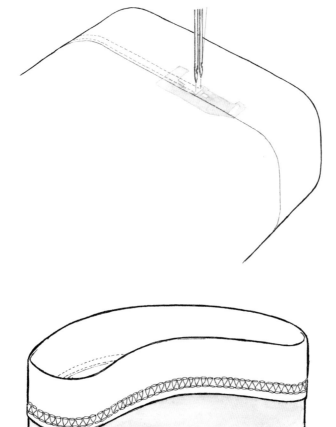

COVER-STITCHED HEM

The beauty of a cover-stitched hem is that it finishes the raw edge of the hem allowance as it applies perfectly parallel rows of topstitching—this finish is neat and speedy!

1. Set the serger for a cover stitch. You may have to attach a special plate that covers the knives. Disengage the upper knife and disable the upper looper.

2. Fold under the hem. If desired, fuse the hem in place with a strip of fusible web so it's easier to catch the allowance when stitching.

3. With chalk or a disappearing marker, mark the location of the hem allowance edge on the right side of the hem. With the right side up, position the fabric so that the left needle enters the fabric on the mark.

4. If you are sewing a circular hem, stop after several inches (centimeters) of stitching and pull the needle threads to the wrong side with a pin—or pull on the looper threads. Resume stitching and serge over the beginning stitches for about 1″ (2.5 cm). Secure the threads, as described below.

ENDING AND SECURING THE COVER STITCH

The cover stitch unravels easily, so unless the ends are enclosed in a seam or caught in an intersecting seam, you need to secure them. Before removing the cover-stitched fabric from the serger, clear the threads from the stitch finger (see page 63). Pinch the fabric and threads together behind the needle to keep the stitch from pulling out as you remove the fabric from the serger. Leave thread tails several inches (centimeters) long.

securing loose thread ends: First, move the needle thread tails to the wrong side of the fabric by gently pulling the looper threads to the left, so the needle threads come through to the wrong side of the fabric. Then, pull the needle threads so they lock with the looper thread. Knot all the threads and dab them with seam sealant or thread them through the stitches.

DECORATIVE COVER STITCHING

You can cover stitch anywhere you like on your project, because the knives are disengaged and won't cut away your fabric. Experiment to discover the many exciting options this versatile stitch offers. You can work with either the right or wrong side of the stitch on view for different effects.

❖ Practice serging decorative threads on fabric scraps.

❖ Mark placement lines on whatever side of the fabric will be placed right-side up during cover stitching. If you're stitching multiple parallel rows, you might be able to use the edge of the presser foot as a guide.

❖ Select the wider needle position when working with thicker threads. For finer threads, either width will do.

❖ Tighten the thread tension for thinner threads; loosen it for heavier threads.

❖ Increase the impact of the stitch by working with decorative, shiny, or metallic thread in the looper. Position the wrong side of the stitch on the right side of the fabric.

❖ Create a decorative, braidlike effect by setting the stitch length so that the stitches meet, with minimal fabric visible between the looper threads.

❖ Stitch as much of the decorative stitching as possible before you start the construction of your project.

❖ Stabilize lightweight fabrics if necessary by placing a piece of tear-away stabilizer on the wrong side of the fabric under the stitching area.

DECORATIVE IDEAS FOR COVER STITCH

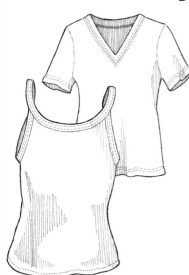

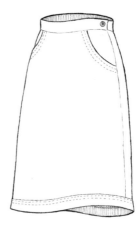

• Topstitch a neckband with the stitching below the seam or with the seam between the two rows of cover stitching.

• Try adding three parallel rows of stitching if your serger has this capability.

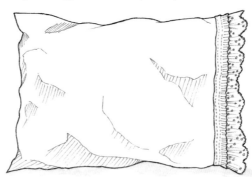

• Fold the hem edge to the right side and cover-stitch it in place to create a novelty finish.

• Bind the edge of a knit top and finish tiny straps without risk of pulling or distorting the fabric.

• Attach edging trim with the cover stitch.

FLATLOCK TECHNIQUES

The flatlock stitch is a decorative, reversible stitch. It is used to topstitch or to create a flat seam in which the seam allowances abut or just barely overlap each other. It is essential that at least half the stitch width extends beyond the edge or fold of the fabric. The heavier the fabric, the more the stitch needs to extend.

The flatlock stitch is made by adjusting the two-thread overedge stitch or the three-thread overlock (see pages 45 and 50 respectively). It's often worked with decorative threads in the looper(s). To set up your machine, refer to your owner's manual and the stitch formation information on page 47. Practice flatlocking with your project fabric and thread. If you aren't pleased with the stitch formation, try again with different color threads, so you can see which threads you think need to be adjusted.

Stitch slowly, guiding the fabric edge. Remove the fabric from the serger and pull the fold flat or pull the fabric edges so they meet. Don't press or force the seam allowances to flatten them; they need to flatten on their own. If they don't, try again with the stitches extending slightly more beyond the fabric edge. In a successful stitch, the loops on the right side and the ladders on the reverse side appear to be the same width.

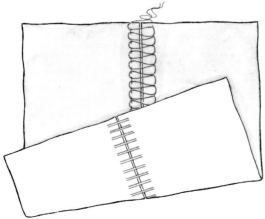

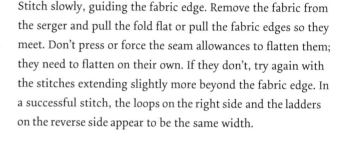

FLATLOCKING BASICS

- Flatlock on knits and nonraveling woven fabrics.

- Choose the flatlock stitch for low-stress seams.

- Install the standard presser foot and disengage the upper blade.

- Start with a longer-than-normal stitch length (about 3 mm [1/8"]) if you are using heavy decorative thread. If you are using fine thread, a shorter stitch length will be fine.

- Work with the left needle to create a wide stitch, which is suitable for decorative flatlocking. If you are attaching lace or working with lingerie fabric, choose a narrow stitch and work with the right needle.

- Use decorative thread in the upper looper to create a stitch with the greatest visual impact.

- Flatlock with the wrong sides of the fabric together if you want the loops to show on the right side of the fabric.

- Flatlock with the right sides of the fabric together if you want the ladder stitches to show on the right side of the fabric.

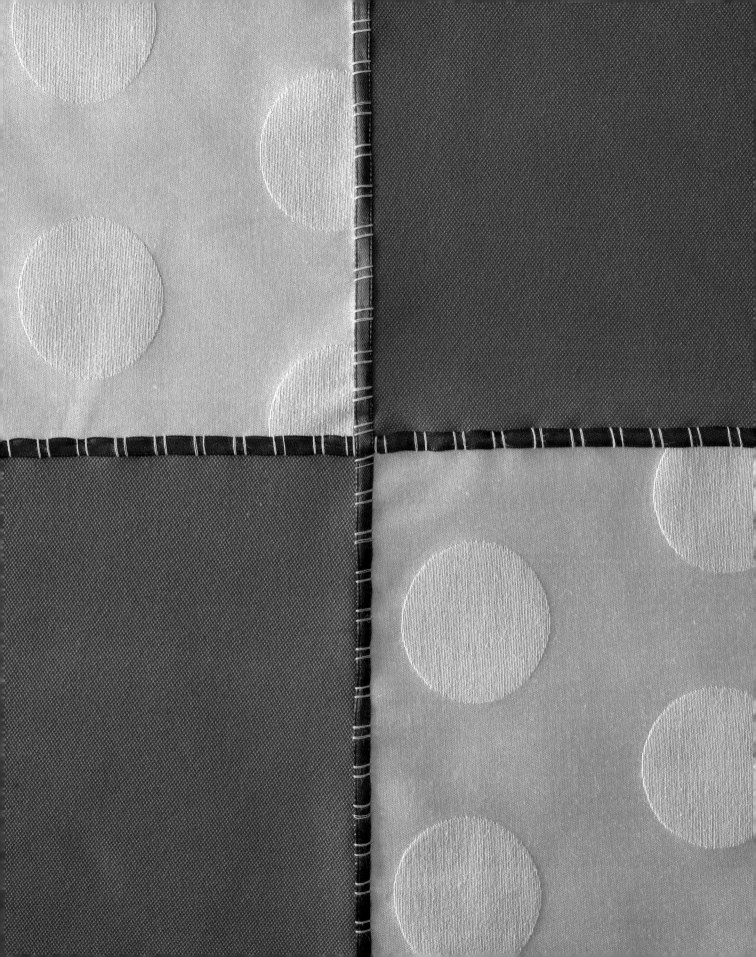

FLATLOCKED SEAMS AND TOPSTITCHING

When you flatlock a seam, the stitches lie over the raw fabric edges. When you flatlock along a fabric fold, you create a line of topstitching.

flatlocked seams: Avoid flatlocking seams on close-fitting garments. A flatlocked seam adds about 1/4″ to 3/8″ (6 mm to 1 cm) to the width of the garment. If you do want a flatlocked seam on a close-fitting garment, mark a new needle stitching line between 1/4″ and 3/8″ (6 mm and 1 cm) to the left of the original seamline. Trim the seam allowance accordingly.

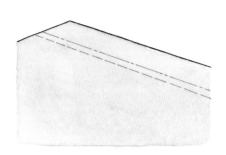

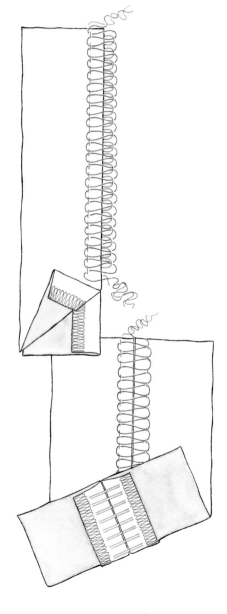

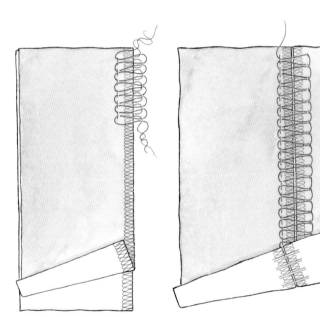

If the fabric ravels, finish the edges with a three-thread overlock before flatlocking.

If the fabric ravels and/or stretches excessively, press the finished edges to the wrong side and flatlock so that the pressed edges abut.

If the fabric is lightweight, the cut edges can overlap slightly without causing too much bulk.

flatlocked topstitching: If you flatlock over a folded edge and then open the fold you will see that you've created a topstitched effect. This technique is a great way to showcase decorative thread. Because there's no cutting involved, you can try flat-locked topstitching anywhere within your project.

Set the serger for a wide, three-thread flatlock and thread the upper looper with decorative thread. Fold the fabric along the desired stitching line. Place the fabric under the presser foot so the needle is about 1/4″ (6 mm) from the edge of the fold. Stitch slowly, letting the stitches extend halfway off the fabric. Unfold the fabric so the stitches flatten.

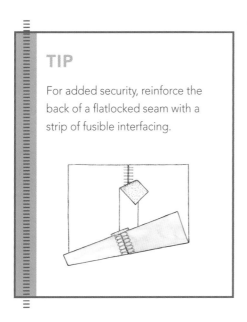

TIP

For added security, reinforce the back of a flatlocked seam with a strip of fusible interfacing.

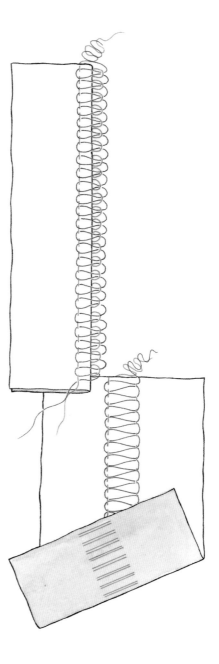

DECORATIVE FLATLOCKING

Flatlocking offers some decorative alternatives to the regular overlock stitch. Keep in mind that the stitches are exposed, so don't position them in an area where they might be easily snagged. To use the flatlock stitch to apply cording or narrow trim, see the couching technique on page 103.

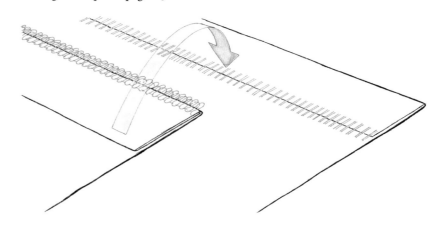

double-fold hem: If you want the loops visible on the right side of your project, press the hem allowance to the wrong side. If you want the ladder stitches visible on the right side of your project, press the hem allowance to the right side. Fold the raw hem edge in to meet the hem fold. Press. Flatlock along the bottom fold, catching the raw hem edge in the stitching. Open the hem and gently pull the fabric flat. Lightly steam-press.

fringed hem: First, you need to decide how long you want to make your fringe. Next, pull a thread to find the straight grain. Or, mark a placement line that is the desired fringe length from the raw edge. At the pulled thread or placement line, press the hem allowance—press it under if you want the loops visible on right side of the project; to the right side if you want the ladder stitches visible on the right side of the project (**A**). Flatlock along the fold. Open the hem and pull the fabric flat (**B**). Carefully remove the threads below the flatlock stitches to create the fringe (**C**).

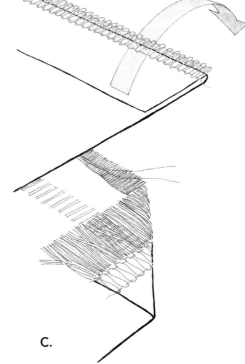

B.

C.

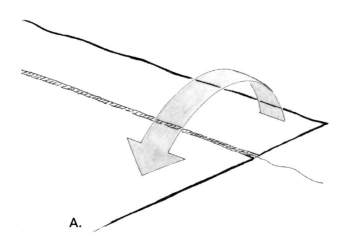

A.

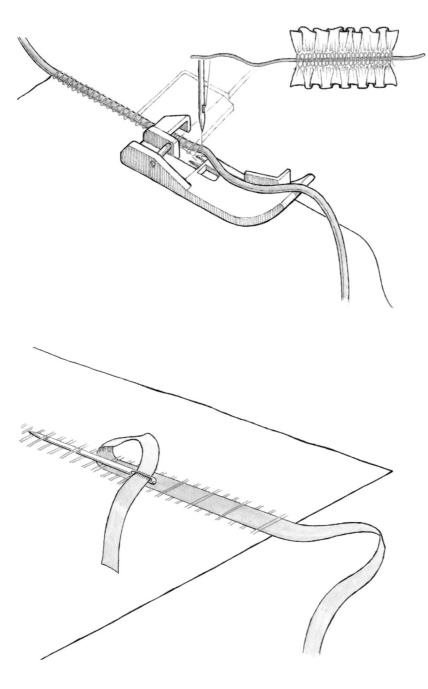

gathering: You can gather fabric by flatlocking over a piece of elastic, cording, or elastic cord. Mark the desired location for the line of gathering and fold the fabric on the mark. Flatlock along the fold, over the elastic or cording. Open the fabric and pull the cording or elastic to gather the fabric. Experiment with placing the elastic on the right and wrong sides of the fabric to see which effect you like best for your project.

A tape presser foot is helpful, but you can work with a standard presser foot (see page 21). Feed the ribbon or cord over the front and under the back of the foot.

thread casing: Create a woven trim effect by flatlocking along a fold so that the ladder stitches are on the right side of the fabric. Thread ribbon, yarn, or gimp in a tapestry needle and weave it in and out of the stitches.

Embellishments and Specialty Fabrics

Decorative Serging

Experiment with your serger. You'll be amazed at how much you can do. Novelty threads make stitching stand out; monofilament threads make it invisible. With some simple stitch adjustments, you can expand the range of decorative possibilities!

BEADING

With a beading presser foot, you can attach strands of beads, pearls, or sequins to a flat fabric surface. This type of decorative stitching works best on a straight or gently curved stitching line. Fold the fabric with wrong sides together along the placement line. Thread the serger with monofilament thread so the stitches are invisible. Set the machine for a two- or three-thread flatlock stitch. A two-thread stitch is better because there are fewer threads to show or wrap around the beads.

Place the string of beads (or pearls) into the groove of the presser foot so they extend slightly behind and in front of the foot, to start stitching over the beads alone. Hand-walk the serger to take the few first stitches. Then, place the fabric under the presser foot and flatlock along the fold.

The looper threads should wrap around the sides of the beads. Stitch slowly. Secure the ends by knotting the threads or using seam sealant.

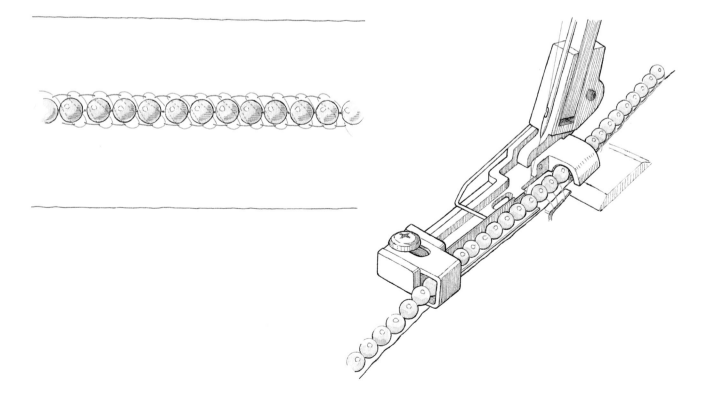

COUCHING

Couching is a method of attaching narrow, relatively flat trim (such as cording, sequins, braid, yarn, and ribbon) to the surface of the fabric. Depending on how you arrange the fabric and trim, the loops or the ladders will be visible over the trim. Be sure that the material you are couching in place is narrow enough to fit between the needle and the lower knife. Disengage the knives to avoid nicking the fabric.

Set your serger for a two-thread flatlock stitch. If your machine has multiple needles, use the one on the far left. Adjust the stitch to a medium-to-long stitch length and a medium stitch width. These adjustments vary depending on the fabric and trim, so be sure to practice the stitching on scrap fabric first.

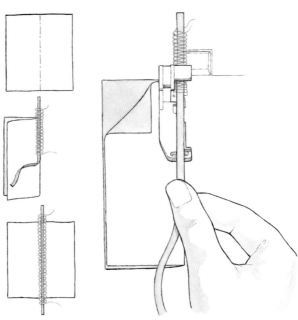

loops on top: Draw placement lines on the right side of the fabric (straight or gently curved lines are best). With wrong sides together, fold the fabric along a placement line. Lift the presser foot and slide the couching material under so it comes out behind the foot and over the top of the front, to the right of the needle. Lower the presser foot and take several stitches, holding the couching material in both the front and back. Place the folded fabric edge just under the tip of the presser foot and under the couching material. Stitch so the stitches extend beyond the fabric fold. Catch the couching material within the stitches (but don't stitch through the couching material). When you have finished a row, open the fabric flat and smooth the stitches over the trim. Secure the thread ends with liquid seam sealant before you continue.

ladders on top: Draw placement lines on the wrong side of the fabric (A). Fold the fabric along one line, with right sides together. Insert the couching material between the fabric layers, positioning it very close to the fold.
Place the fabric fold under the toe of the presser foot and flatlock so that at least half of the stitch hangs off the edge of the fabric (B). Don't catch the couching material in the stitching. Open the fabric and secure the ends of the trim with seam sealant (C).

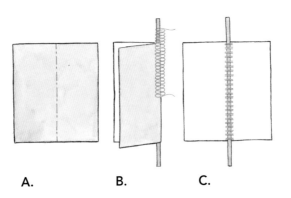

A.   B.   C.

CHAIN AND BRAID TRIMS

A serger can stitch whether or not there's any fabric under the foot—another major difference between the serger and sewing machine. The key to making lengths of trim is to work with decorative thread.

TIP

If you want to add a dash of color to braid trim, overlock over a colorful ribbon or twill tape.

BRAID

Make custom braidlike trim by setting your serger for a three-thread overlock stitch. Cut a piece of tricot (or any clear, flexible fabric) twice as wide as you want the trim, usually between 1/2″ (1.3 cm) and 5/8″ (1.6 cm) wide. Fold the tricot in half and feed it through the slot on a taping or elastic presser foot. You could also start with a precut product, such as Seams Great, instead.

The overlock stitches form over the tricot (which is practically invisible) to create flat trim, which you can then stitch directly onto a garment or other type of project.

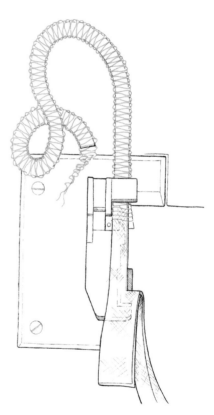

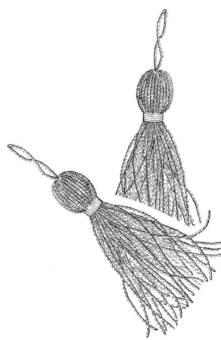

THREAD CHAIN

Without placing any fabric under the foot, set your serger for a rolled edge and serge away. Make the chain as long as you want. Then use the chain to make a tassel, a button loop, or an applied trim. The weight of the thread determines the chain's diameter. Pearl cotton makes lovely chain.

DECORATIVE EDGINGS

Serging is a perfect way to finish fabric edges, and there are many ways to turn basic serger stitches into decorative edgings. Refer to the section on decorative rolled edges, for even more ideas (see page 89).

DECORATIVE THREAD

The easiest way to make an edge finish decorative is by working with special thread (see page 27). As long as the thread has similar weight and the same care requirements as the fabric, you can work with just about any thread you like. Make a test swatch first to adjust the machine settings. Always serge slowly when working with decorative thread so you can control the results.

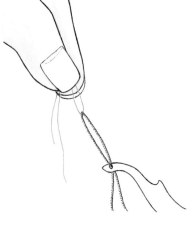

To check that the thread will feed through the loopers smoothly, double a length and thread it through the eye of the looper. If the doubled thread goes through easily, you can use it —if it doesn't, consider couching the thread along the fabric edge instead (see page 103).

> ### TIP
>
> Switch to a large eye needle (100 or 110) if you are using thick decorative thread in the needle.

WIRED EDGE

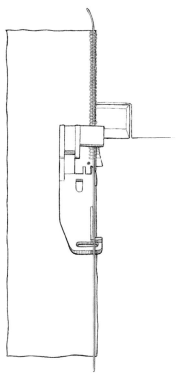

To make flowers or other craft embellishments, just add a wire along the edge of a ribbon or fabric strip so you can shape the fabric into the form you want. Then apply the shaped embellishment directly to the hems of costumes, crinolines, and special-occasion gowns to create structured, decorative shapes.

The wired-edge technique is similar to the technique for a fishline edge (see page 89). For a wired edge, however, you work with a fine, 24-to-30-gauge, rust-proof craft wire and a rolled-edge stitch. Remember to disengage the knives.

Position the wire under the back and over the front of the presser foot, so it is between the needle and the knife. Set your serger for a two- or three-thread rolled edge with a short and narrow stitch. Stitch, with the fabric under the wire, encasing the wire in the stitching. If you're working with fabric, trim a little off the edge. If you are adding wire to ribbon or another type of trim, don't trim away fabric as you serge the wire in place.

PIPED EDGES

It's easy to make your own piping with a serger. You can cover cording with fabric. Or you can cover filler cord with thread.

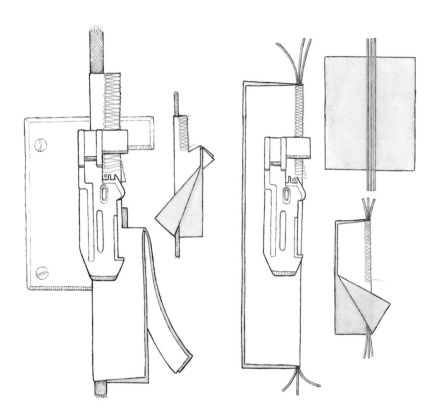

fabric piping: Cut bias strips of fabric wide enough to cover the cording plus 1 1/4″ (3 cm) for seam allowances, and long enough for the length needed. Fold the fabric strip lengthwise, with wrong sides together, with the cotton cording inside the fold. Attach a cording presser foot and position the piping in front of the presser foot with the fabric raw edges to the right and the cording in the groove of the foot. Stitch with a three-thread overlock stitch. The seam holds the cord in place, and the overlock stitches finish the flange.

thread-covered piping: By working with a chiffon base (or any lightweight, sheer fabric), you can make piping in any thread color you like. Cut bias strips of chiffon 2″ (5.1 cm) wide by the desired length. Place narrow filler cord or several lengths of pearl cotton in the center of the chiffon strip. Fold the chiffon in half over the cord. Thread the serger with thread in the desired piping color. Disengage the knives and serge over the filler cord with a three- or four-thread overlock stitch. The stitches form your custom piping, and the fabric makes a flange for attaching the piping to your project.

attaching piping to a single fabric layer: Position the serged edge of the piping along the cut edge of the fabric with the right side of the fabric facing up. Attach a cording foot and serge the piping to the fabric with the cording in the groove of the presser foot and a three- or four-thread overlock stitch.

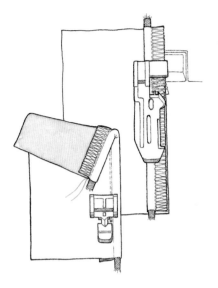

Fold the serged seam allowance to the wrong side so the piping extends out from the fabric. Anchor the serged seam allowance to the project by chainstitching or straight-stitching on a sewing machine.

sandwiching piping between two layers: Position the piping between two pieces of fabric (right sides together); position the piping's serged edge slightly away from the cut fabric edges. Attach a cording foot and feed the three layers together through the serger, with the cording in the groove of the presser foot, using a three-, four-, or five-thread overlock stitch.

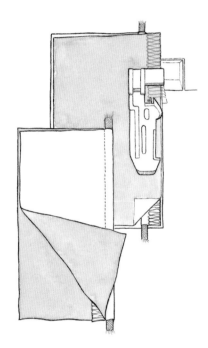

APPLIED EDGE TRIM

To attach lace or any trim that has one straight and one decorative edge to a fabric edge, position the straight edge of the trim along the fabric edge with right sides together. Serge with a short, narrow, three-thread overlock stitch. Press the trim away from the project and the seam allowance toward it.

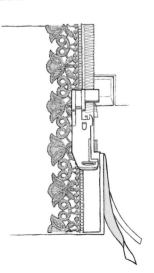

HEIRLOOM SERGING

The term *heirloom* describes feminine, Victorian-inspired clothing and accessories—think delicate blouses, christening gowns, handkerchiefs, and elegant cotton nightgowns. Heirloom garments have lots of ruffles, entredeux, pintucks, lace insertions, and fabric puffing. All of these decorative embellishments once had to be stitched painstakingly by hand, but now it's incredibly easy to create the same effects with a serger.

To achieve an authentic heirloom look, work with delicate fabrics, such as organdy, batiste, and satin, in shades of white, ecru, or pastel. Heirloom trims are usually the same color as the fabric, creating an elegant monochromatic look, although ribbon weaving and embroidery offer the opportunity to introduce soft hints of pastel colors. Make sure the thread you use is the same weight as the fabric; for lightweight fabrics, choose finer thread. Rayon thread adds a hint of shine, and soft pink thread adds subtle contrast. Always make a test sample to ensure that the fabric, thread, and trim are compatible.

Heirloom style is defined by the type of trims you choose and how you combine them. Here is a description of the most popular heirloom trims.

❖ *Entredeux* is narrow trim with wide holes. It may take several forms: a narrow strip with holes; a narrow strip with fabric borders for attachment to the project; or a narrow strip of holes along the edges of other trims.

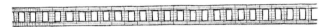

❖ *Beading* is a narrow lace or embroidered trim that has openings that you can weave ribbon through.

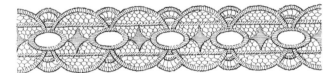

❖ *Lace edging* has one straight edge, for attaching to a fabric edge, and one decorative edge that extends beyond the fabric edge.

❖ *Insertion* lace has two straight edges and it is sewn between other trims or between pieces of fabric.

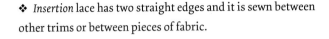
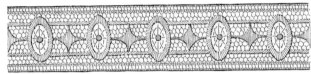

❖ *Eyelet* and *embroideries* are useful trims if they are narrow with at least one straight edge.

❖ A fabric *puffing strip* is gathered on both long edges and inserted between two other trims or pieces of fabric.

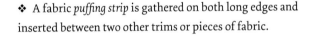
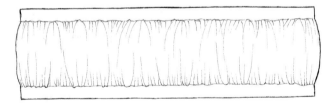

PLANNING THE DESIGN

To design a beautiful heirloom project, plan ahead. Cut the pattern piece you want to embellish from plain muslin or paper. Lay out your collection of laces, entredeux, ribbons, and other trims, using the muslin or paper to make sure you have collected enough of each. Arrange the embellishments until you like the composition. If you want to include pintucks, you'll need to include fashion fabric between the laces and trims.

Next, stitch all the elements together to form an heirloom "fabric" that's larger than the pattern piece. Lay your pattern on the heirloom fabric and cut it out, just as you would a plain piece of fabric. After cutting, secure the ends of all the joining seams with seam sealant.

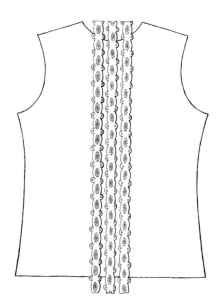

JOINING TRIMS AND FABRIC STRIPS

A two-thread flatlock stitch is the best choice for joining most heirloom elements. It forms a flat, almost invisible seam. It's important to practice with scraps of trim before you start making the fabric. Try using monofilament or fine embroidery threads for nearly invisible stitches. Or, for a subtle hint of color, use a slightly heavier colored thread or rayon thread; the stitches then become part of the design.

entredeux: The key to serging entredeux to any other trim or to fabric is to make sure that the needle enters each hole once. Adjust the stitch width and length carefully. Place the entredeux and fabric or trim with right sides together and edges aligned. If you are stitching to fabric, position the entredeux so a little sliver of fabric extends beyond it; this way, the serger blade will trim it as you stitch. This extra bit of seam allowance strengthens the seam. Flatlock the two layers together. Gently pull the stitches flat and press.

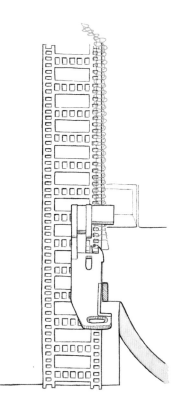

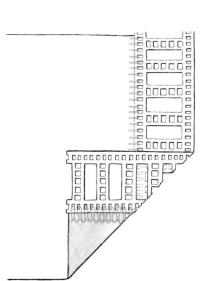

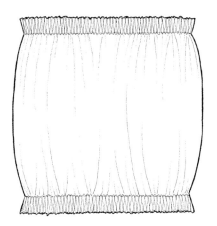

TIP

Spray starch adds body to the trims and laces, which makes them easier to work with.

lace edging, beading, and lace insertion: Use a two-thread flatlock (for a very flat seam) or a two- or three-thread rolled edge to attach straight trim edges to fabric or to each other. Practice first to make sure the seam is flat. Place the two layers with right sides together and serge along the edge with short, narrow stitches. Press the seam flat. If you are working with insertion trim, repeat the process on the opposite side. If you are attaching beading, weave narrow ribbon in and out of the holes after the beading is stitched in place.

fabric puffing strips: Prepare the puffing strips by cutting your fashion fabric as wide as desired and two to three times the desired finished length. (Cut it two times the desired finished length for a slightly puffy finish and three times for a fuller puffing strip.)

You can use the differential-feed feature to gather both sides of the strip to the desired length. Or you can cut a second fabric strip to the desired finished length and width. Gather each long edge of the longer strip so it is the same length as the shorter strip (see page 78). You can also gather the puffing strip directly to the other piece in one step (see page 79). With right sides together, serge both long edges of the strips with a four-thread overlock. Turn the strip right side out. Then attach the double-layer strip to other elements or to a garment.

FAGOTING

Fagoting is a technique often used to attach lace trims in heirloom-style clothing. It's a type of flatlock seam in which the fabric edges don't meet under the flatlock stitches. Fagoting is only a decorative technique and isn't suitable for construction.

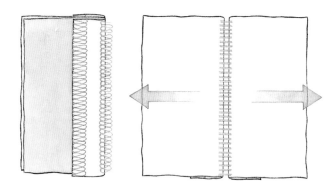

Set your serger for a two-thread flatlock stitch and disengage the knives. A two-thread flatlock stitch is better than a three-thread stitch because the threads pull flatter. Edge-finish the raw edges of the two pieces you'll be joining. Press under 1/2″ to 5/8″ (1.3 to 1.6 cm) seam allowances. With right sides together, stitch the two pieces with the flatlock stitches extending slightly more than halfway off the folded edges. Practice first to determine how much you need the stitches to extend to create an attractive effect. Gently pull the two pieces apart so the stitches appear between them and then press.

PINTUCKS

Set your machine for a rolled hem. The stitch width determines the width of the tuck. Mark placement lines on flat fabric and press along the markings. Try to keep the pintucks on the straight grain and about 3/4″ (1.9 cm) apart. With wrong sides together, lightly press the fabric along the placement lines. Serge. Keep the fabric fold close to but not touching the knife. Serge all the pintucks in the same direction to avoid distortion and to ensure that the top of the stitch always shows on the same side. Press the pintucks softly to one side and secure the thread ends.

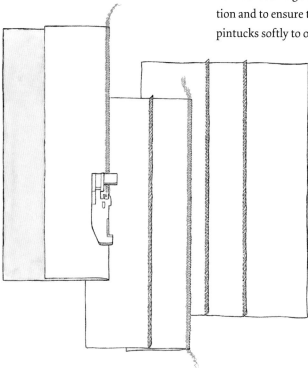

SHIRRING

Shirring is made up of multiple rows of gathering that create a smocked look—an easy effect to achieve with the serger. You'll work with elastic cord to gather the fabric. There are two great ways to add shirring to a garment: with a chain stitch or an overlock stitch. Both techniques require that you mark placement lines. Stitch at least three rows to make nice-looking shirring. Disengage the knives as you'll be stitching away from the edge of the fabric.

CHAIN-STITCH SHIRRING

Set your serger for the chain stitch and thread the chain-stitch looper with elastic thread. Use regular sewing thread in the needle. Position the fabric right side up and serge along the marked line. Stitch the remaining lines, stretching the fabric so it's flat during serging. If the fabric is heavy and you want more gathers, set the differential feed to gather.

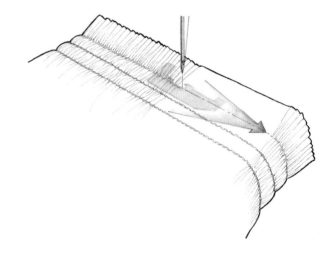

OVERLOCK SHIRRING

Set your serger for a short, medium-width, three-thread overlock stitch. Fold the fabric with right sides together along the first placement line. Place a piece of elastic cord under the back and over the front of the presser foot. Overlock-stitch over the cord. At the end of the row, pull the cord behind the needle and chain off. Cut the cord, leaving about 3″ (7.6 cm).

Serge elastic cord along the remaining marked lines. Pull the elastic cords together to shirr the fabric to the desired width. Knot the cords at each end.

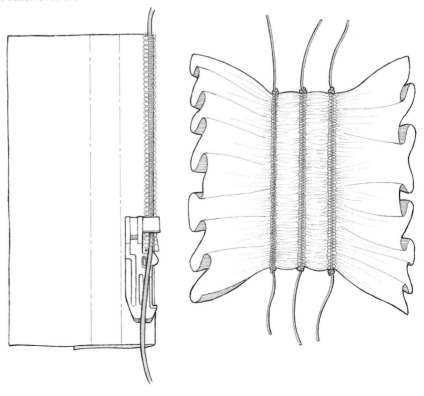

TOPSTITCHING

Any serger that can form a chain stitch can also topstitch—and just think of the different threads you can use! Mark topstitching lines on the garment or fabric with tailor's chalk. Disengage the knife and set the serger for the chain stitch. Experiment with a variety of novelty threads for different effects. If the thread is heavy, use it in the looper. Then sew with the right side of the fabric down so the decorative chain stitch appears on the right side.

RIBBING BANDS AND EDGES

Ribbing is the stretchy knit fabric with vertical ribs applied to the hems and necklines of T-shirts, sweatshirts, sweat pants, and some fashion garments. Ribbing stretches so the wearer can easily get the garment on and off. The garment edge then returns to its original size for a neat look and comfortable fit. Ribbing is almost always attached with a serger because the serger stitch stretches with the ribbing and forms a seam that is narrow and free of bulk.

TYPES OF RIBBING

Ribbing can be purchased as tubular yardage, from 24″ to 60″ (61 cm to 1.5 m) wide. It is also sold in pre-folded strips or bands (with wrong sides together) that are between 1″ (2.5 cm) and 4″ (10.2 cm) wide. The raw edges of the bands are serged to the garment, with the folded edge finishing the garment.

Ribbing is also available in many types of fibers. The key is choosing ribbing with the greatest resilience (which is also called recovery), the property that allows it to stretch but then quickly return to its original shape and length. The addition of spandex in the ribbing increases resilience. Wool is another fiber that stretches and recovers nicely. Match the care requirements and weight of both the fabric and the ribbing. Be sure to give the ribbing a test stretch before you buy it to make sure it bounces back nicely.

TIP

Don't preshrink ribbing. Shrinking doesn't affect the size, and washing removes the sizing, making the ribbing difficult to serge.

WIDTH AND LENGTH OF RIBBING

Ribbing bands can be as wide as you want, but they are typically narrower at necklines than at hems. Typically neckbands are less than 2″ (5.1 cm) wide. Hem bands are less than 4″ (10.2 cm) wide.

The length of the band is determined by the edge it is being attached to. For a body-hugging band, cut the ribbing shorter than the garment opening and stretch it as you serge. In most cases, cut the ribbing between two-thirds and three-quarters the size of the garment opening. To make sure the ribbing fits over your head, wrists, or ankles, pin the band ends together and slip on the garment.

ATTACHING RIBBING

There are two basic ways to attach ribbing: with the garment flat or with the garment already sewn. Flat construction is simpler. You can make a sweatshirt or top in next to no time. If the garment is already sewn, you attach the ribbing to a stitched circular opening, which produces smoother joins at the openings. In either case, set your serger for a three- or four-thread overlock stitch with a medium stitch length and width.

flat construction of a jewel-neck T-shirt: It's easiest to attach the ribbing before you sew the garment together, especially if you're sewing a small garment. Always work with the right sides of the fabric together, with 1/2″ (1.3 cm) seam allowances, and with the ribbing on top of the fabric so you can stretch it.

1. Serge one shoulder seam. Divide and pin-mark the neckline and the ribbing band into quarters. With right sides together, pin the raw edges of the ribbing band to the garment edge, matching the pins. The garment opening is larger than the rib band. Serge the ribbing to the garment, stretching the ribbing and removing the pins as you serge.

2. Serge the other shoulder seam, up to and through the neckline ribbing band. Hide the thread tail (see page 64). Attach the sleeves. Serge ribbing to both sleeve hems with right sides together.

3. Serge the underarm and side seams on one side, in a single pass.

4. Serge ribbing to the bottom edge with right sides together. Then serge the remaining underarm and side seams. Bury all the thread tails.

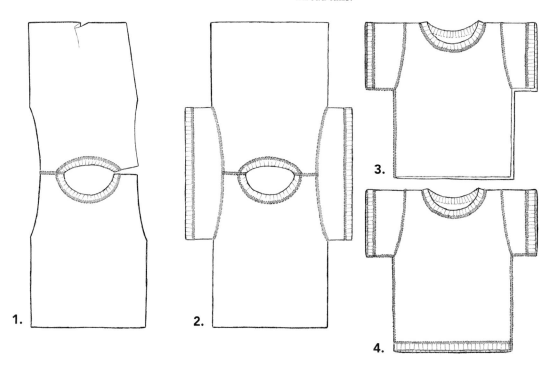

1.

2.

3.

4.

flat construction of V-neck ribbing

1. Serge one shoulder seam. Staystitch (that is, machine-stitch just inside the seamline) the point of the V neckline to strengthen it.

2. Clip into the V, up to but not through the stitching. Serge the ribbing to the neckline by opening the neckline so it is straight (see inside corner technique, page 71). Work with the fabric on top, so you are sure to catch the fabric at the V in the seam.

3. At the center of the front neckline, fold the rib trim in half with the right sides together. With a sewing machine or by hand, stitch diagonally from the serged stitches to the edges of the ribbing. Clip the miter fold, so you can press it, and hand-sew the flaps of the ribbing down. Press lightly.

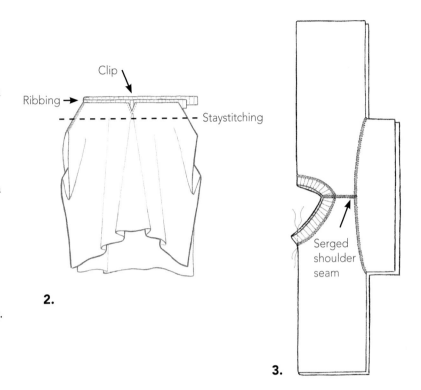

2.

3.

circular construction of ribbing

1. Cut the ribbing to the desired size. With right sides of the short edges together, serge the ribbing into a circle. Fold the ribbing in half with wrong sides together. Sew both shoulder seams. Divide and pin-mark the ribbing and neckline opening into quarters.

2. With right sides together, pin the ribbing to the neckline opening, matching pins and placing the ribbing seam in the center back. Serge the seam, stretching the ribbing and removing the pins as you serge. End the seam by overlapping the stitching and tapering the stitch off the edge.

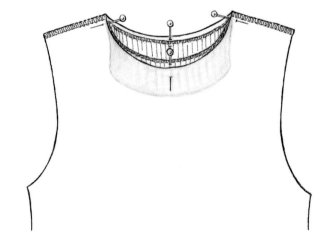

Specialty Fabrics

Your serger is so versatile you can work with a wide array of specialty fabrics—lace, satins, sheers, and even fur! One of the great advantages of the serger is the way it handles knit fabrics and finishes their edges. It also hems slippery fabrics easily, with a professional rolled hem. Sheer fabrics look fabulous with narrow overlocked seams.

Here is a brief guide to working with the fabrics that you might have avoided because they were too problematic to sew. With your serger, they're no problem at all!

KNIT AND STRETCH-WOVEN FABRICS

The serger makes sewing stretch fabric easy because the serger stitch stretches just as much as the fabric does. Here are some general guidelines for success:

❖ Install a size 70/10 or 80/12 universal needle; if the stitches skip, switch to a ballpoint needle.

❖ Set your serger for a three- or four-thread overlock stitch for most seaming.

❖ Choose an all-purpose polyester or cotton/polyester thread. For very stretchy fabrics, consider textured nylon thread.

❖ Engage the differential feed function to prevent wavy edges (see page 37). If your serger doesn't have a differential feed, ease the fabric through the presser foot, as described on page 70.

❖ Stabilize horizontal or stressed seams to prevent them from stretching out of shape. The shoulder and the crotch seams benefit from the addition of a piece of twill tape. There are three ways to stabilize a seam:

1. Fuse knit interfacing along the seam to stabilize the fabric while retaining some stretch.
2. Catch twill tape, seam tape, or ribbon in the seam to minimize stretch.
3. Catch clear elastic in the seam. It will stretch, but it will recover its shape.

❖ For Lycra, use a new needle; choose wooly nylon thread, which stretches a lot; set the serger for a wide three- or four-thread overlock stitch.

❖ For tricot, use a new needle to prevent snags, pulls, and skipped stitches; work with stretch thread or with decorative threads in low-stress areas; guide the fabric under the presser foot to start; set up for a narrow three-thread overlock stitch, a rolled hem, or flatlock stitch.

❖ For sweater knits, use a four-thread or five-thread safety stitch to prevent these knits from stretching out of shape; engage the differential feed to control these unstable fabrics; hem with a cover stitch.

SHEER FABRICS

The narrow overlock seam or rolled-edge seam is perfect for sheer fabrics. Both are almost invisible from the right side and they don't have a lot of bulk. Always start with a new, size 70/10 or 75/11 needle and change it often. A shorter stitch length, differential feed, and/or taut serging also make it easy to serge these special fabrics and to avoid puckered seams (see page 70).

LACE AND OTHER TEXTURED FABRICS

Fabrics with surface texture can cause uneven stitching. Avoid decorative stitching on these types of fabrics and try to plan seams between rows of texture, if possible. For textured lace, shorten the stitch length and narrow the stitch width. Taut sewing and differential feed minimize puckered seams. If the lace has a lot of open areas, include a strip of tricot bias binding in the seam to add surface area for the serger stitches.

HEAVYWEIGHT AND BULKY FABRICS

You can jeopardize the mechanics of your serger by trying to feed very thick fabrics between the knives. Try to compress thick fabrics like boiled wool, polar fleece, and velvet before you stitch. Sew a row of straight or zigzag stitches near the cut edge with a sewing machine. Then, serge so that the knives cut directly on top of the row of stitching.

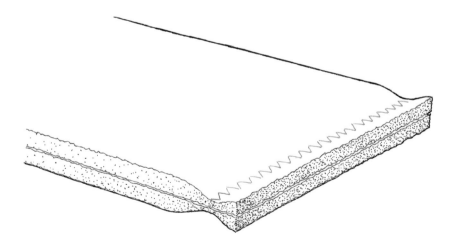

FAKE AND REAL FUR

Fur, whether fake or real, is too bulky to fit through the serger, but you can flatlock-stitch layers together. First, trim away the seam allowances and brush the fur away from the edges. Flatlock the edges with right sides together. Pull the two pieces open and flat. Use a tapestry needle to fluff the pile that might be caught in the stitch. You also might want to reinforce the seam with a piece of fusible tape on the wrong side, covering the stitches.

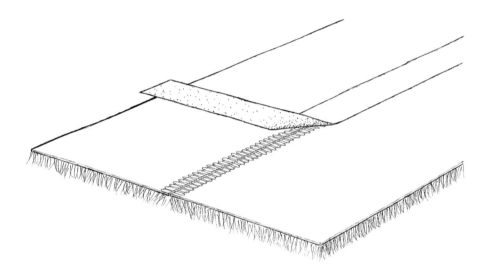

SLIPPERY AND SATIN-FINISH FABRICS

Although the differential feed feature minimizes wavy edges and puckered seams, satin fabrics will still shift and slip. You might need to baste the seams together before stitching. If the fabric layers shift just as you are starting to serge, lift the presser foot and position the beginning of the seam under the foot to hold the layers together. The best way to hem these fabrics is to serge a rolled edge—perfect every time!

Quick Fixes and Tips

TOP TEN SECRETS TO SUCCESS

1. Fit your garment before you serge.

2. Always test-serge on scrap fabric before beginning your project.

3. When in doubt, rethread. Most stitching problems are solved by rethreading. Loosen the tension dials when threading. Always thread in the correct order.

4. Never serge over pins.

5. If you only need to use one needle for a stitch, remove those that won't be used.

6. Change needles frequently. Be sure to use the right-sized needle for the weight of your fabric.

7. Leave the presser foot lowered when you start and finish serging. Leave at least a 3" (7.6 cm) thread chain on the serger to prevent thread jams.

8. Make sure the knives are either fully engaged or completely disengaged, depending on the type of stitch.

9. Keep the looper doors closed.

10. Don't pull the fabric as you're serging—just guide it gently.

COMMON STITCH PROBLEMS AND SOLUTIONS	
PROBLEM	**SUGGESTED SOLUTION**
Poor stitch quality	Make sure needles are inserted properly. Choose better-quality thread. Change to different type and/or size needle. Check thread tension. Avoid heavily textured fabric.
Skipped stitches	Change to different type and/or size needle. Loosen needle(s) or looper(s) tension. Prewash fabric to remove fabric finish. Avoid pulling fabric during stitching. Reinsert needle(s). If fabric is heavy, increase presser-foot pressure, increase stitch length and width, or choose larger needle.
Thread breaks	Check thread paths; rethread in proper order. Loosen tension on the thread that breaks. Check that needle(s) are inserted properly. Change to a different type and/or size needle.
Needle breaks	Install new needle properly (all the way into needle clamp). Make sure new needle isn't bent. Avoid pulling fabric. If fabric is heavy, stitch slowly. Use a larger needle. Loosen thread tensions.
Fabric puckers	Use and adjust differential feed. Hold fabric taut (see page 70). Shorten stitch length. Loosen needle tensions. Stitch slowly.
Jagged fabric edge	Trim more off fabric edge, at least 1/8" (3 mm). Shorten stitch length. Change to heavier thread. Check alignment of knives.

COMMON STITCH PROBLEMS AND SOLUTIONS

PROBLEM	SUGGESTED SOLUTION
Fabric jams	Watch for tangled threads, which can pull fabric into serger. Make sure trimmed fabric doesn't fall into looper area. Make sure thread, fabric, and stitch are compatible. Check that knives are in correct positions. Hold thread tails toward the back when beginning to serge. Change to less bulky fabric or compress layers (see page 122). Lengthen stitch. Loosen looper tensions.
Fabric stretches	Use and adjust differential feed. Trim more off fabric edge, at least 1/8" (3 mm). Lengthen stitch length. Ease—do not pull—fabric (see page 70). Stabilize fabric edge with spray starch or stabilizer. Decrease presser foot pressure.
Stitches hang off fabric edge	Decrease stitch width. Adjust position of upper knife.
Fabric bunches under stitches	Increase stitch width. Check that knives are activated.
Fabric curls under stitches	Increase stitch width. Decrease cutting width of knives. Loosen looper tensions.
Knives not cutting properly	Make sure knives are in correct positions. If necessary, replace blades. If fabric is lightweight, add spray starch or stabilizer.
Needle holes visible at seamline	Switch to smaller needle size or ballpoint needle. Use finer thread.
Decorative threads feed unevenly	Use horizontal spool holder.

TROUBLESHOOTING GUIDE

If you encounter any problems while serging, don't panic. Just check this list of easy-to-fix problems.

❖ Be sure the serger is plugged in and turned on.

❖ Make sure the serger is on a smooth, steady surface so it doesn't rattle and make strange noises or feed unevenly.

❖ Extend the thread pole completely and check that thread isn't wrapped around or snagged on a spool holder. Also check for tangled or caught thread anywhere on the serger.

❖ Check that the serger is ready to go, the looper doors are closed, the presser foot is down, the presser foot is properly attached, and the correct stitch finger is in position.

❖ Remove the needle(s). If they are old, replace them. Otherwise, re-insert them to make sure they are inserted correctly. Check the needle chart on page 18 to make sure that you are using the right needle for the fabric.

If you are still having trouble, make sure the serger is threaded correctly. Check each thread path to make sure that the thread hasn't slipped out of a thread carrier. Be sure the needles and loopers are threaded from front to back (or back to front—whichever your manual indicates is correct for your machine). Check that the threads are feeding smoothly off the thread spools.

If you still haven't found the source of the problem, make a few stitch samples with different tension adjustments to be sure the tension is right for your stitch. Also consider replacing the thread; poor-quality thread can cause poor stitch quality. If the serger still isn't stitching properly, unthread the machine completely (all threads) and rethread it, following your owner's manual and taking care to thread each path in the correct order. See pages 42–43 for how to adjust thread tensions and pages 28–31 for more information about threading.

MACHINE CARE AND MAINTENANCE

The most important way to keep your serger running smoothly is to clean it, removing lint and bits of fabric after each use. Lint tends to build up under the throat plate, within the looper area, and between the knife blades. Dust your serger with the brush included in the accessory package or with a small, soft bristle paintbrush or make-up brush. A mini vacuum, sold with sewing machine and serger supplies, is a great way to suck lint and fabric right out of the machine. You can also clean the machine with canned, ozone-safe, compressed air, but be careful that you blow the lint out of rather than into the motor.

DUST THE DISKS

Periodically, it's a good idea to clean dust from between the tension disks, too—especially if you are experiencing stitch or tension problems. Turn all the tension dials to their lowest setting or, if possible, release the thread tensions completely. If you have canned air that has a mini straw that allows you to direct the air into narrow spaces, use the straw to clean between the disks (always read the instructions on the label first). You can also fold a clean piece of tightly woven fabric in half and slide the folded edge between the disks.

OIL

Not every serger needs to be oiled. Check your owner's manual. The manual will tell you whether or not your serger requires oiling, what type of oil to use, where to put it, and how often to oil. The standard rule indicates that machines that require oiling should be oiled after eight to ten hours of serging or whenever you hear any metallic scraping sounds. You may also want to oil your serger if it hasn't been used for a long time.

REPLACE THE KNIVES

Serger knives cannot be sharpened, but fortunately they don't dull easily. Typically, you'll only need to replace knives if you hit a pin or after many hours of serging. Your owner's manual will tell you how to replace the blade on your specific machine. Usually an extra blade is included in the accessory package.

CHANGE NEEDLES

A bent, dull, or burred needle will cause skipped stitches. You'll probably hear a clicking or punching sound when the needle needs to be changed. Just as you would with your sewing machine, get in the habit of replacing your needles fairly frequently. If the needle is new and the stitch quality isn't right, change the size or type of needle until you get the result you're after.

CHECK THE PARTS

If you use and love your serger, you might want to treat it to a routine checkup with the dealer. As with all machinery, checking the moving parts regularly is always a good way to be sure your serger is operating at its best.

BUYING GUIDE AND CONSIDERATIONS

Whether you are buying your first serger or looking to upgrade to a new machine, do a little homework before you go shopping. There are lots of sergers to choose from, and new ones come on the market all the time. If you have a sewing machine that you like, check out the sergers made by that same manufacturer—chances are good you'll like that product, too. Spend time comparison shopping on the Internet. You should also test drive two or three different brands. They all look and feel slightly different and function differently, too.

Take a test drive. It provides a great opportunity for a sales person to give you an overview and teach you about the best features of the machine. Make sure you are comfortable operating the machine. If you can, try serging with different weights of fabrics, to get a good feel for the machine.

Everyone has different priorities and preferences, of course, but certain serger features are fundamental. Here's a list of the essential features to explore when you are shopping:

❖ Number of threads and type of stitches available

❖ Method for converting to different stitches (especially rolled-edge stitches)

❖ Ease of threading

❖ Method for differential feed adjustment

❖ Electronic foot control

❖ Built-in thread cutters

❖ Novelty presser feet, with easy on and off

❖ Ease of tension adjustment

❖ Stitch finger location and ease of adjustment

❖ Ease of adjusting stitch width and length, cutting width, and presser foot pressure

❖ Type of knives (movable or stationary)

❖ Cover stitch capability

❖ Chain stitch capability

❖ Computerized stitch selection and machine settings

❖ Size of sewing area

❖ Number and type of accessories included

❖ Terms of warranty

❖ Option for lessons

❖ Cost

❖ Clarity of instruction manual

INDEX